in associa[illegible]
pr[illegible]

What We Did To Weinstein

by Ryan Craig

First performed at the Menier Chocolate Factory
Wednesday 21 September 2005

Menier Chocolate Factory
53 Southwark Street
London
SE1 1RU

www.menierchocolatefactory.com

Cast in order of appearance

Josh	**Josh Cohen**
Officer / Waiter	**Matthew Burgess**
Yasmin / Samira	**Vineeta Rishi**
Max	**Harry Towb**
Sam	**Leonard Fenton**
Sara	**Miranda Pleasence**
Yusef / Tariq	**Pushpinder Chani**

Creative Team

Director	**Tim Supple**
Designer	**Simon Scullion**
Lighting designer	**Jackie Shemesh**
Composers	**Lemez Lovas** and **Yaniv Fridel**
Producers	**David Babani** and **Danielle Tarento**

Menier Chocolate Factory from 21 September
to 12 November 2005

CAST

Matthew Burgess Officer / Waiter

Trained at The Guildhall School of Music and Drama.
Theatre includes: *Omma* (King's Head), *A Midsummer Night's Dream* (Wild Thyme, Globe Theatre, Neuss, Germany), *Voyages* (Jet Theatre, Croydon Warehouse), *Dealing with Clair* (Union Theatre), *Romeo and Juliet* (Wild Thyme, UK tour), *The Girl With The Almond Eyes* (Theatre Venture), *Three Servants* (Jet Theatre, Croydon Warehouse and tour), *City Boys* (Soho Theatre).
Television includes: *London's Burning* (ITV), *The Mrs Bradley Mysteries* (BBC), *The Stretch* (Sky), *D-Day, The Untold Story* (BBC).
In 2004, Matt received a Fox Scholarship enabling him to spend five months on the island of Bali studying traditional forms of mask and dance-drama.

Pushpinder Chani Yusef / Tariq

Trained at Carlton TV Workshops and the Birmingham Theatre School.
Theatre includes: Orsino in *Twelfth Night* (The Stage Works), Joe d'Costa in *Midnight's Children* (RSC), Tansen in *Baiju Bawra* (Theatre Royal Stratford East), *14 Songs, 2 Weddings and a Funeral* (Tamasha Theatre Co), Jay in *Made in India* (Leicester Haymarket Studio), Tony / Mike in *Adoption* (Birmingham Rep), Tripitaka in *Monkey Magic* (Midlands Arts Centre). He has also done extensive Theatre in Education.
Television includes: *Life Isn't All Ha Ha Hee Hee, Casualty, Doctors* (all BBC).
Film includes: *Cross My Heart* (Filmfour), *Anita and Me*.
Radio includes: *Ties, A Minus, Behind Closed Doors* (all Radio 4), *Silver Street* (BBC Asian Network).

Josh Cohen Josh

Trained at LAMDA.
Theatre includes: *The Graduate* (Gielgud Theatre), *Rent* (Shaftesbury Theatre), *A Chaste Maide in Cheapside* (with the Almeida), *Phallacy* (Kings Head), *Quartermaine's Terms* (Salisbury Playhouse).
Film & TV includes: *The Lost Battalion* (for A&E), *Fire* (for TNT), *The Murder Rooms* (BBC).

Leonard Fenton Sam

Extensive repertory theatre, including work at the Citizens, Glasgow, and the Traverse, Edinburgh, where he performed in Beckett and Pinter. Leonard toured in *The Long and The Short and The Tall* with Michael Caine and Terence Stamp. He also played Bardolph to Orson Welles' Falstaff in the film *Chimes at Midnight*. In London, he appeared with the RSC, the RNT and at the Royal Court Theatre, where he played in *Happy Days* with Billie Whitelaw, directed by Samuel Beckett. Other notable London appearances: *A Midsummer Night's Dream* at the Almeida, directed by Jonathan Miller, *Saint's Day* (Orange Tree), *The Square, The Bespoke Overcoat* and *The Irish Hebrew Lesson*.
Television includes: Dr Legg in *EastEnders* (BBC), Erich Gottleib in *Shine on Harvey Moon, Z Cars, Colditz, The Fourth Arm*.
Film includes, most recently, *The Bride* with Andrea Corr (nominated at the Hollywood Short Film Festival).

Miranda Pleasence Sara

Theatre includes: *Crossing Jerusalem* (Tricycle Theatre), *Simpatico* (Royal Court), *Thatcher's Children* (Bristol Old Vic), *Burning Issues* (Hampstead), *Backpacker Orpheus* (Sound Theatre).
Television includes: *Wonderful You* (ITV), *The Tenant of Wildfell Hall* (BBC), *The Jury* (BBC), *Touch of Frost* (ITV), *Shockers* (Channel 4), *New Tricks* (ITV), *Rosemary and Thyme* (ITV).
Film includes: *The Affair of the Necklace, The Announcement, Safe Haven.*

Vineeta Rishi Yasmin / Samira

Trained at Mountview Academy of Theatre Arts.
Theatre includes: *Beasts and Beauties* (Bristol Old Vic), *Hobson's Choice* (Young Vic), *The Firebird* (Midlands Art Centre), *Beyond The Wall and Over The Sea* (Leicester Haymarket), *The Tempest* (1399 Theatre Co – open air), *Picture Me* (Red Ladder Theatre Co).
Television includes: *The Last Detective, Lawless, The Bill, Doctors.*
Vineeta also plays regular character Jodie Howard in the BBC Asian Network's radio soap, *Silver Street.*

Harry Towb Max

Harry comes from Belfast. His first London appearance was at the Arts Theatre in *The Gentleman Gunman*. Many West End productions include: *Fairy Tales of New York, Little Shop of Horrors, Anything Goes, Barmizvah Boy, Brighton Beach Memoirs, Man and Superman, The Home Place.* For the RSC: *Section Nine, The Iceman Cometh, Sherlock Holmes, Travesties.* For the RNT: *Guys and Dolls, Death of a Salesman, Angels in America, Macbeth, Edmond, His Girl Friday, The Mandate, A Funny Thing Happened on the Way to the Forum.* For the Abbey Theatre, Dublin: *Philadelphia Here I Come, The Rivals, The Importance of Being Earnest.* He made his Broadway debut opposite Shelley Winters in Saul Bellow's *Under the Weather.*
Hundreds of TV credits from early *Z Cars* to *Heartbeat.*
Many films credits include: *Above Us the Waves, The 39 Steps, Patton, The Blue Max.*
Writing credits include documentaries and radio plays and he has written and read over 20 of his own short stories for BBC Radio 4.

CREATIVES

Tim Supple Director

Tim is Co-Director of DASH and has directed and adapted theatre and opera throughout Europe, North and South America and the Middle and Far East.
As Artistic Director of the Young Vic (1993–2000): *Oedipus, The Slab Boys Trilogy, Grimm Tales* (Time Out Award), *The Jungle Book, Blood Wedding, More Grimm Tales, Twelfth Night, As I Lay Dying, A Servant to Two Masters.* For the RSC: *Spring Awakening* (1995), *The Comedy of Errors* (1996), *Tales from Ovid* (1999), *Love in a Wood* (2001), *Midnight's Children* (2003). For the National Theatre: *Whale* (1989), *Accidental Death of an Anarchist* (1990 – Olivier Award nomination), *Billy Liar* (1992), *The Epic of Gilgamesh* (1993), *Haroun and the Sea of Stories* (1998).
Opera work includes new versions of *Hansel and Gretel* (2001) and *The Magic Flute* (2003) for Opera North and *Babette's Feast* (2002 and 2004) for the Linbury Studio, ROH.
Tim has recently directed two films: *Twelfth Night* (Projector / Channel 4 – also adapted, BAFTA nomination) and *Rockabye* (IWC / Channel 4).
In 2005/6 Tim will direct *A Midsummer Night's Dream* in India to tour the sub-Continent and the UK, visiting Stratford as part of the RSC's Complete Works Festival.

Ryan Craig Writer

Plays include: *Broken Road* (Edinburgh Fringe, winner of a Fringe First), *Portugal* (National Theatre Studio), *Three Servants* (Warehouse), *Happy Savages* (Lyric Studio), *Sins of Dalia Baumgarten* (Etcetera).
Television includes: *Night and Day* (ITV), *Hollyoaks* (Channel 4), *Mile High* (Sky One), *Dream Team* (Sky One), *Family Affairs* (Channel 5).
Ryan is writer in residence at BBC Radio Drama. His radio work includes: *Looking For Danny, Portugal,* and the series *The Great Pursuit.*

Simon Scullion Designer

Trained at Wimbledon School of Art and was a finalist in the Linbury Prize for Theatre Design.
Theatre work includes: *Blue Room* directed by Joe Harmston (national tour), *Messiah* directed by Stephen Berkoff (Edinburgh Festival), *Organillo* for Stephen Mottram's *Animata, Fair Mind of the West* directed by Andy Goldberg and *Zipp!* directed by Carole Todd (Duchess Theatre).

Jackie Shemesh Lighting Designer

Graduated from Jerusalem School of Visual Theater.
His works in dance include various pieces for the Batsheva Ensemble between 1995 and 2004. For Gizela Rocha Company, Zurich: *Go Behind* (2002), *Love Hate Reason and Me* (2003). For Constansa Macras, Berlin: *Big In Bombay* (2004). For Yasmeen Godder, Tel Aviv: *Hall* (2002), *Two Playful Pink* (2003), *Strawberry Cream and Gunpowder* (2004).
Theatre productions include: *Othello* (1997, Haifa Theatre), *Place With Pigs, Life Is a Dream* (1995, London). He has designed works for many other theatre, dance and opera companies in Israel.

Music works include artists such as Ehud Banay (1996–2005), Meira Asher / Den Haag: *Spears Into Hooks* and *Infantry*, Arik Hayut, Berlin, Rona Keinan, Josef Sprinzak and composer Keren Rozenbaum in Tel Aviv.
Upcoming productions include: *Glass House* (Uri Ivgi, Norrdance Company, Sweden) and *The Town of The Little People* (Ofira Henig, Hahan Theatre, Jerusalem).

Lemez Lovas Composer

For the BBC World Service: presented/co-produced a documentary for Masterpiece; *The Orange Revolution* (2005), *The Voice, part 2* (2005).
Head of Music at Openair Radio, University of London (2003). Head of Late Night Music at Oxygen 107.9 FM, Oxford, and presenter/producer of the weekly programme (1996–7).
Theatre work includes: *Watch* (also on Radio 4), *God of Vengeance* (Camden People's Theatre, 2001), *Hunting of the Snark* (Crazy Horse Theatre Company at the Museum of London, 2000).
Film score credits include: *Small Blood Drive Victories* (ZDF, Germany with Nik Ammar), *Romantik* (2003, Turkey), *Sitting Ducks* (2003), *Sanhedrin* (UK 2003), *Talking Tacheles* (A C Films, 2002).
Recordings: currently working on a compilation for Trikont Records, Germany. *Ticking Again* (Kharkov Klezmer Band, Music & Words, NL, 2003 – producer), *Laughter Through Tears, Digital Folklore* (Oi Va Voi, 2002).
As musical director: *Radio Gagarin – Experiments in Sunday Socialism* (Notting Hill Arts Club).
Lemez is also DJ at the bi-monthly 'Costa Urbana' night at the Notting Hill Arts Club.

Yaniv Fridel Composer

Yaniv is a producer, multi-instrumentalist, theatre composer, song writer. His music can be described as atmospheric, romantic and uplifting, combining contemporary electronic sounds and live instruments.
To date, Yaniv has composed more than 10 dance and theatre shows, numerous TV and film productions and ad campaigns. His album recently was top demo in *Sound on Sound* magazine.
Yaniv has worked with Scapino ballet, Tim Supple, Israeli Philharmonic Orchestra, ensemble Bat-Sheva, dANTE OR dIE theatre, CNN, Oi Va Voi, Pinedrop and other artists.

David Babani Producer

David is Artistic Director of the Menier Chocolate Factory, where productions have included: *Tick, Tick...Boom!* by Jonathan Larson, *Murder* by Anthony Shaffer, *Fully Committed* by Becky Mode (winner of Best Overall Fringe Production 2005, TheatreGoers' Choice Award) and subsequent transfer to the West End (Arts Theatre), *Americana Absurdum* by Brian Parks. As Artistic Director of the Jermyn Street Theatre, he produced *Simply Barbara*, which broke all box office records, transferred to the Playhouse Theatre and toured internationally, and the critically acclaimed production of *Closer Than Ever* by Maltby and Shire. In Australia, David produced the world premiere of *Symphonic Forbidden Broadway* and international concerts with Jason Robet Brown, Andrew Lippa and Maltby and Shire, all at the Adelaide Cabaret Festival. Other productions include *Forbidden Broadway* (Albery Theatre), *The Donkey*

Show (Hanover Grand), the international hit comedy, *The English American* by Alison Larkin (Soho Theatre), *Boom Chicago* (Jermyn Street, Soho Theatre, Royal Festival Hall) and a hugely successful production of Stephen Sondheim's *Assassins* (New End).

Danielle Tarento Producer

Danielle trained as an actress and appeared in a diverse range of roles, from highbrow theatre at the Almeida to very highbrow TV such as *Dream Team* for Sky One. She associate-produced *Tamburlaine the Great* at the Rose Theatre in 2003, the first production to be staged there in over 400 years. Since taking over the Menier Chocolate Factory, she has produced all the in-house productions with David Babani, as well as managing the adjoining restaurant and bar.

WHAT WE DID TO WEINSTEIN

First published in 2005 by Oberon Books Ltd
521 Caledonian Road, London N7 9RH
Tel: 020 7607 3637 / Fax: 020 7607 3629
e-mail: info@oberonbooks.com
www.oberonbooks.com

A catalogue record for this book is available from the British Library.

ISBN: 1 84002 581 6

Printed in Great Britain by Antony Rowe Ltd, Chippenham

Characters

JOSH, twenty four to thirty two

OFFICER, early twenties

YASMIN, twenty

MAX, early seventies

SAM, early seventies

SARA, twenty four to thirty two

WAITER, early twenties

YUSEF, early twenties

TARIQ, early twenties

SAMIRA, twenty

OFFICER and WAITER should be played by the same actor

YUSEF and TARIQ should be played by the same actor

YASMIN and SAMIRA should be played by the same actor

Setting: West London and The West Bank

The time runs back and forth between 1994 and 2002

Hate traps us by binding us too tightly to our adversary.
This is the obscenity of war.

Milan Kundera

ACT ONE

Scene 1

The stage should be fairly bare. Essentially it is a room which contains a bed, a table and some chairs and maybe a sort of side table, all of which can be moved. There should be a liquidity to the piece. Scenes should run into each other.

Lights up on JOSH, staring ahead in a holding cell. An army OFFICER in the Israeli Defence Force – mid-twenties, but confident and powerful, enters holding a file / dossier.

OFFICER: Let's go over this report again. OK? So I can understand.

JOSH: (*Nothing.*)

OFFICER: Your unit was making an incursion into the West Bank.

JOSH: (*Nothing.*)

OFFICER: There was a dog fight and you became separated from your unit. Yes?

JOSH: (*Nothing.*)

OFFICER: On the road from Qalqilya to Tulkarem, along the Green Line, you came across a lone man breaking the curfew. You captured him. You tied his hands. You blindfolded him and you requested he kneel. You followed the guidelines to the letter up till then, as always. Well done.

JOSH: (*Nothing.*)

OFFICER: You radioed in. You were given orders. Do you remember what they were?

JOSH: (*Nothing.*)

OFFICER: You committed a serious breach, you know that, a serious offence.

JOSH: (*Nothing.*)

OFFICER: Help me to understand why you did it.

JOSH: (*Nothing.*)

OFFICER: (*Smiles, changing tack.*) I read that story you wrote.

JOSH: (*Nothing.*)

OFFICER: About your father.

JOSH: (*Nothing.*)

OFFICER: I found it interesting. I'd like to talk about it with you.

JOSH: (*Nothing.*)

OFFICER: I'd like to talk about what you meant by it.

JOSH looks at the OFFICER.

I'd like to talk about…if it has anything to do with what happened today.

JOSH looks confused.

If it has anything to do with…why you lost control.

JOSH: (*Nothing.*)

OFFICER: You see. We do care. We're not total monsters.

OFFICER smiles. JOSH walks forward.

We'll take things into consideration is what I'm saying, but you must, you absolutely must…talk to me.

Lights up a bit. We are now in a West London hospice. A room with an empty bed. This is JOSH thinking back and will happen throughout. The OFFICER steps back into the darkness, while YASMIN, a nurse, enters.

YASMIN: (*Seeing JOSH.*) Hello.

YASMIN opens the curtains in the room. During the next exchange she is busy bringing the bed forwards and arranging the room from cell to hospital room.

JOSH: I'm Josh.

YASMIN: Good for you.

JOSH: Uh…yeah, I'm looking for Max Pepper. They told me room 302.

YASMIN: This is 302.

JOSH: (*Checks his watch.*) It's not easy to find is it?

YASMIN: Did you have trouble?

JOSH: I got a bit lost actually. It's very poorly signposted isn't it?

YASMIN: Well you're here now and that's the main thing.

JOSH: Where is he anyway? I'm on a tight schedule.

YASMIN: I think he's revolting.

JOSH: What?

YASMIN: I think he's…

JOSH: Look, I know he's got some bad habits, but he's an old man…

YASMIN: No. I mean as in 'rising up in revolt'.

JOSH: Oh. Right. What?

YASMIN: He is a feisty one, isn't he?

JOSH: Yes, yes he is, did you say he was 'rising up in revolt'?

YASMIN: Oh he's always at it, bless him. He incites the other residents to chant outside the manager's office. How do you know him again?

JOSH: What?

YASMIN: He usually tells me about his friends.

JOSH: Is there anyone I can speak to?

YASMIN: Are you one of his poker school?

JOSH: No, I…look…poker school?

YASMIN: He didn't mention a Josh though.

JOSH: Right.

YASMIN: I'm sure I would have remembered.

JOSH: He didn't mention me?

YASMIN: I've read some of his books.

JOSH: Short stories.

YASMIN: Have you?

JOSH: It's been a while to be honest.

YASMIN: Me too. I did them at school. Syllabus.

JOSH: I know.

YASMIN: He's quite famous.

JOSH: (*Looking outside.*) Yeah, look is there anyone else I could speak to…

YASMIN: You know, I think he's working on something at the moment. I often see him writing.

JOSH: (*Back to YASMIN.*) What?

YASMIN: I've never looked after a celebrity.

JOSH: Did you say he was writing?

YASMIN: I sometimes catch him scribbling away when I'm on nights. Oh, no, I don't let him see me. I've got a theory, would you like to hear it?

JOSH: Yes. No. Look…

YASMIN: I think he's writing his memoirs.

JOSH: (*Beat.*) His memoirs?

YASMIN: I mean he's got some amazing stories about his life. The politics, the affairs with actresses…Actually I think he's at it with one of the female residents, the dirty old perve. How do you know him again?

JOSH: … I'm his son.

YASMIN: … Hello.

JOSH: I'm Josh.

YASMIN: Yes. Josh. Of course… Hello.

JOSH: I thought he hadn't mentioned me?

YASMIN: …maybe he did and I just forgot.

JOSH: Yuh. I was due to meet him in his room at seven.

YASMIN: I'll just go and see if they're done revolting.

YASMIN exits. OFFICER steps out of the darkness.

OFFICER: You were a good soldier. You were loyal. Patriotic. Then you publish this story. What happened? Did something happen on your trip home to England? Did something happen with your father?

JOSH looks at OFFICER who steps back into the darkness.

YASMIN wheels on MAX. He is in a wheelchair. He is dressed in pyjamas and a dressing gown. He has a mane of white hair and a white beard.

JOSH: You look like God.

YASMIN goes about folding the sheets of the bed down.

YASMIN: Come on Mr Pepper.

YASMIN helps MAX out of his wheelchair and into the bed.

JOSH: King Lear at least. Or Obi-wan Kenobi. I mean the beard. You've grown a beard. I'm not used to the beard. But it's…you know…it's good to see you anyway.

MAX looks at YASMIN and gestures to JOSH.

MAX: Who's this?

YASMIN: This is Josh.

Awkward pause.

JOSH: Or Gandalf.

YASMIN: Yes. *Lord of the Rings*!

MAX: (*Snorts.*) Tolkein? Couldn't write his way out of a paper bag.

A beeper goes off.

YASMIN: Time for your drink.

MAX: Christ.

YASMIN: I won't be long.

YASMIN leaves. Silence. JOSH tries to say something interesting. MAX just stares.

JOSH: So, this is…

MAX: Nurse! Where's that nurse?

JOSH: She said she wouldn't be long.

MAX: Yeah. She said that to me once, I didn't see her for three weeks. I'm telling you the service in here is a fucking disgrace.

JOSH: Oh yeah? Is that why you were revolting?

MAX: What?

JOSH: I asked if that was the reason you were rising up in revolt?

MAX: Oh that. Well. Listen to this one. They let us watch telly between seven in the morning and five in the afternoon. We're forced to watch Daytime TV. You ever hear anything as sadistic as that?

JOSH: Because we were supposed to meet at seven.

MAX: DAYTIME TV. Hateful, witless twits with karaoke grins. It's like being beaten over the head with candy floss. They're trying to neutralise our minds.

JOSH: It's now quarter to eight.

MAX: Yeah. So?

JOSH: So I've been here for half an hour.

MAX: Ah-ha! Gotcha!

JOSH: What?

MAX: So you were late by quarter of an hour?

JOSH: ...technically, yes.

MAX: Well, what have you got to say for yourself?

JOSH: I forgot how exhausting you were.

MAX: I want a cup of tea. NURSE!

JOSH: What are you shouting for?

MAX: Who's shouting? NURSE!

JOSH: Stop it, they'll sedate you.

MAX: NURSE!

JOSH: They'll put you in restraints.

MAX: Let them try. I'll bite their bloody hands off. NURSE!

JOSH: I heard you were writing.

Stop. Pause. MAX looks sheepish.

Is it true?

MAX: (*Pause.*) What do you mean you heard?

JOSH: What's it about?

MAX: You don't want to listen to what you heard.

JOSH: What's the theme?

MAX: What have I always told you? 'Never listen…to… what you hear.' Yeah.

JOSH: No, what you used to say was 'do as I say, not as I do'.

MAX: Did I? Well. That's very good advice.

Re-enter YASMIN.

YASMIN: Here we go Mr Pepper. Drink this up.

MAX: Ooh. Happy hour already?

YASMIN: Come on, open wide.

MAX: Not today thank you.

YASMIN: D'you want me to get tough with you?

MAX: Yeah? You want a piece of me?

YASMIN: Drink your medicine.

MAX: I want a cup of tea! Whose uncle do you have to be to get a cup of tea in this hole?

YASMIN: Open up for me now and I'll get you a cup of tea.

MAX succumbs. He opens his mouth and YASMIN pours the drink into it.

There. That wasn't so difficult was it?

MAX: (*Swallows and grimaces.*) Tastes like battery acid.

JOSH: How do you know what battery acid tastes like?

MAX: There's a lot you don't know about me, son.

JOSH: So you admit I'm your son?

YASMIN: (*Looks embarrassed.*) I'll go and get that tea.

MAX: And don't over-brew.

YASMIN: I'll tell the chef.

YASMIN leaves.

MAX: She always over-brews. It's like drinking battery acid.

JOSH: You said that already.

MAX: What?

JOSH: You used that joke already. You're repeating yourself.

MAX: I've got three months to live, you want me to come up with new material now?

Pause. JOSH smiles sadly.

I suppose you've seen your mother.

JOSH: Of course. She seems happy.

MAX: (*Utter contempt.*) With Sheldon?

JOSH: He's not so bad.

MAX: He sells flags. Flags! And his name's Sheldon for fuck's sake.

JOSH: He's doing well, Sheldon. Flags are on the up.

MAX: How can she be happy with a man called Sheldon who sells flags?

JOSH: What's wrong with flags?

MAX: I heard a rumour they go barn-dancing together. I mean for the love of Christ.

JOSH: I think you mean line-dancing.

MAX: Barn-dancing, line-dancing, they dress up in hats and boots and wave flags. I mean I ask you, in the name of everything decent. (*Beat.*) But you know your mother, she won't be told.

JOSH: (*Beat. Hurtful.*) Like I say. She seems happy.

MAX: Yeah. Well. I mean I…me and your mum, we…

JOSH: …well…

MAX: She wanted to be free. What could I do?

Beat. Re-enter YASMIN with tea.

YASMIN: Here's your lightly brewed tea.

MAX takes the tea and stares at it.

MAX: What the fucking hell is that?

YASMIN: There was no Tetley's left so you've got… I think it's…ginseng and camomile.

MAX: Ginseng and camomile? I'm dying, I'm not a lesbian. Take it away.

He gives it back. YASMIN puts the cup on the table without flinching and starts plumping up MAX's pillows.

JOSH: Look, I have to go.

MAX: (*Sudden fury.*) Easy with those pillows girl! What have I told you?

JOSH: I have to meet someone.

MAX: So go. What do I care?

JOSH: I'll be back tomorrow.

MAX: So I'll see you tomorrow. If I make it that long. (*Beat. JOSH doesn't move.*) He's still here. Why is he still here?

JOSH: I suppose I could phone her and say I'll be another half an hour…

MAX: Go. Go. You're cluttering up the room. Go.

JOSH: If you'd been here at the agreed time…

MAX: Right. (*He starts to get out of bed.*) I'll go and meet her. Where is she?

YASMIN: (*Gently pushing him back into the bed.*) You're not going anywhere mister.

JOSH: Stop it. I'm going, OK?

MAX: Go. You never needed my permission.

JOSH: Just, I…

MAX: …to, to gallivant half way across the world.

JOSH: Dad…

MAX: I don't remember you asking my permission to do that.

JOSH: No.

MAX: Which I wouldn't have given by the way, as you very well know.

JOSH: Yes.

MAX: You knew my feelings on the subject very well. Very well.

JOSH: The world knew your feelings on the subject. You made them very public.

MAX: So why did you do it? Why did you go?

JOSH: Because I had my own feelings on the subject.

MAX: You defied me. You betrayed me.

JOSH: At least I didn't… (*Stops himself.*)

Beat.

MAX: At least you didn't what? Say it.

JOSH: Nothing.

MAX: At least I didn't what?

There's a stand-off. Finally…

JOSH: I have to go.

Beat. JOSH steps back into the darkness. YASMIN raises her eyebrows.

MAX: He takes after his mother.

YASMIN: Get some rest.

YASMIN goes to leave.

MAX: I know you watch me.

YASMIN turns at the door.

When I'm writing… I can see you out of the corner of my eye.

YASMIN: Oh. I…

MAX: It's all right.

YASMIN: I don't mean to be…

MAX: Do something for me. (*MAX takes out some pages from under his pillow.*) If I die…

YASMIN: Mr Pepper. Seriously, I…

MAX: Listen to me. If I die before I'm done, promise me… promise me…you won't let him get his hands on this.

YASMIN: Who?

MAX: My son. Don't let him get hold of this. Promise me.

YASMIN: It's not really my job to…

MAX: It's important. Promise me.

YASMIN: OK.

YASMIN leaves.

OFFICER: It's tough for all of us in this country. After all, we are at war. And the truth is: we're on our own. Israel is alone and always has been. We have only each other.

MAX takes some pages from under his pillow and reads them. Then he pulls a pen out of his top pocket and begins to write. JOSH is watching this.

If we can't trust each other, who can we trust?

JOSH: (*Nothing.*)

Darkness.

Scene 2

Restaurant / bar. SAM and SARA have just finished their meals. They sit in silence. Finally…

SAM: Did I tell you…? Your Mum tried to read one of your reports the other day.

SARA: … *Tried?*

SAM: Drove all the way out to Colindale to buy the paper.

SARA: For God's sake, why?

SAM: Didn't want anyone to see her. Sat in some caff. Saw your photo and wept.

SARA: Did she read it?

SAM: Sat there sobbing. In Colindale!

SARA: …did she actually *read* my article?

SAM: She couldn't see through the tears.

SARA: Mum's being very hard on me you know? I ring home…as soon as she hears my voice…you know…she puts the phone down.

SAM: Because of your articles.

SARA: Which she doesn't read.

SAM: She's blinded by the tears.

Pause. SAM takes out his wallet and rifles through it.

SARA: Um…

SAM: Sorry?

SARA: What are you doing?

SAM: Eh?

SARA: What are you doing with that?

SAM: This?

SARA: I thought we agreed…

SAM: What? I'm just checking I've got enough cash.

SARA: I thought we agreed this was my treat.

SAM: You were being *serious*?

SARA: I… Put that away please.

SAM: Don't be ridiculous…

SARA: Dad.

SARA glares at him. Beat. SAM puts his wallet back in his pocket.

Thank you.

SAM: Also. Your mother sent me with a question.

SARA: Right. Did she? The answer's no.

SAM: You haven't even heard the question.

SARA: She wants to know my *situation.*

SAM: You're no spring chicken. Mid-thirties.

SARA: I'm thirty two.

SAM: Bit long in the tooth to be fancy free.

SARA: I need another drink.

SARA looks over for a waiter.

SAM: What happened to that fella you were seeing? The Chiropodist.

SARA: (*Calling off.*) Excuse me!

SAM: He was harmless.

SARA: Yes. Also gay.

SAM: Gay?

SARA: I know.

SAM: Gay? He was huge.

SARA: I was surprised too.

SAM: He was gay?

SARA: (*Looking for the waiter.*) Where's that guy?

SAM: Well…at least he was a professional.

SARA: What?

SAM: He made a living didn't he? He'd have looked after you.

SARA: … What? Dad…

SAM: What? You couldn't have worked around it?!

SARA: Worked around it?

The WAITER arrives.

Another glass of red. Large.

SAM: And clear the plates would you?

WAITER: Yeah, I'll do that in a minute.

SAM: What?

WAITER: I'm just having a conversation. OK?

SAM: A conversation?

SARA: And a glass of water.

WAITER: Still or spar…

SAM: Tap. From the tap. The tap.

WAITER: Right. Glass of red and a water. From the *tap.*

WAITER exits.

SAM: (*About WAITER.*) He's got a bit of an attitude hasn't he?

SARA: And, can I say, I don't need looking after. I've got a job. A pretty bloody good job actually.

SAM: You know what I think of that job. The effect it's having on your mother and me.

SARA: (*Sighs.*) Not this again.

SAM: Our friends don't come round. Our…don't invite us out…

SARA: You told me….

SAM: They…

SARA: …you told me…yes, Jesus…

SAM: People avoid me in *shul.*

SARA: Because of my job? Really? Is that really true?

SAM: Yes, it really is. It's really true.

The WAITER appears with the drinks.

WAITER: One glass of red. (*He says this provocatively.*) Large.

WAITER puts down the glass of red.

SARA: Thanks. (*In a rage.*) That kind of petty-minded ignorance makes me fucking furious! (*Soft, to WAITER.*) Could we see the dessert menus please?

WAITER: What? Yeah, all right. And one water. (*Puts down the water.*) Fresh from the tap.

WAITER goes.

SAM: (*About WAITER.*)What did he say?

SARA: Mum hates me.

SAM: Listen, your mother…she's…she loves you. We both do. You're our special princess…our little baby girl…

SARA: Baby? What happened to 'mid-thirties'? You can't have it both ways.

SAM: Maybe you should start behaving like it then.

SARA: Meaning?

SAM: Meaning look at you. Look at that shirt.

SARA: What's wrong with this shirt?

SAM: Nothing wrong with the shirt, it's a very nice shirt.

SARA: So?

SAM: So you got something against the buttons?

SARA: No.

SAM: So you couldn't do some of them up?

SARA: It's hot.

SAM: The whole world has to see your cleavage?!

WAITER arrives. He can't help but look at SARA's chest. She covers it. WAITER takes some plates and goes.

You know you're getting a bit of a reputation in the community.

SARA: The community?

SAM: Things are being said.

SARA: Look... I'm always away. It's hard to, you know, *conduct* a relationship when you're jetting off to some war zone...and, and you don't know when it's going to end...if it ever will. Home for me is more a state of mind than...

SAM: I mean I don't mind if he's not Jewish anymore. Fine. Marry a goy. Marry whoever you like, as long as he can tie his shoe laces, who cares? But all this bouncing from one character to the next... Eddie and *Barnaby* and, and Malcolm, I mean...they can't be all that different from each other can they? They're all blokes. They're fairly similar aren't they?

SARA: Finally we agree on something.

SAM: So pick one and get it over with. What are you doing, some kind of survey?

SARA: Who's Malcolm?

SAM: The one with the teeth.

SARA: Oh *Malcolm*!

SAM: I'm still sorry it never worked out with Josh. He adored you.

SARA: That was a long time ago.

SAM: What happened? It was going so well. Then all of a sudden…

SARA: It just didn't work out. OK? Can we drop it?

SAM: Sure. We'll drop it. (*Beat.*) It kept me up at night. I drove your mother nuts. Nuts. I would nudge her out of a deep sleep, literally nudge her…and you know how your mother hates to be nudged. I'd say, 'Sandra. Sandra. You're a woman. Explain this to me. A person of Josh's calibre, a person who's crazy about her. I thought we all agreed on Josh. You're a woman. Explain this to me from a woman's perspective.' And you know what she says to me? 'Sammy,' she says, 'you're driving me nuts. Shut up.'

WAITER comes over.

WAITER: … Any sweets?

SARA: We haven't decided.

SAM: Where's the toilet, son?

WAITER: Gents, back on the left

SAM goes.

Was everything OK?

SARA: Fine.

Pause.

WAITER: Haven't I…

SARA: Sorry?

WAITER: Sorry.

SARA: No, no, it's OK.

WAITER: I've seen you here before.

SARA: …yes.

WAITER: I thought you looked familiar.

SARA: You recognised me?

WAITER: You don't usually eat.

SARA: What, you mean I usually stagger about drunk?

WAITER: No.

SARA: I'm usually a blabbering wreck?

WAITER: You always look pretty good to me.

SARA: Yeah?

WAITER: Yeah.

SARA: Oh. Well I mean…good then.

WAITER: …anyway, I'd better…

SARA: Yeah.

They hold a look. WAITER exits. SARA smiles and sips her drink. There is a lighting change and all of a sudden we can hear the distant sounds of a party. JOSH, looking smarter and younger than before, enters. He sees SARA.

JOSH: Having fun?

SARA: Are you being sarcastic?

JOSH: I forgot: You hate weddings.

SARA: They give me the creeps. Everyone forcing themselves to have a wonderful time. It's desperate.

JOSH: (*Looking back to where he came from.*) It's actually all right.

SARA: I was watching you before.

JOSH: (*Turning back to her. Smiling.*) Were you?

SARA: Yeah....didn't know you could dance.

JOSH: Oh...just messing about.

SARA: She's very pretty.

JOSH: Yeah. (*Quick beat.*) Sorry, who?

SARA: Your girlfriend.

JOSH: Oh right.

SARA: Whatsername.

JOSH: Yes...her...uhm...Melanie.

SARA: Ah yes, The Lovely Melanie.

They hold a look.

JOSH: I heard you were seeing...

SARA: I am.

JOSH: So?

SARA: He's not Jewish.

JOSH: So?

SARA: So I wouldn't subject the poor boy to a Jewish Wedding.

JOSH: Chris isn't Jewish.

SARA: Chris?

JOSH: My best mate. Chris. You know Chris. Anyway, Chris is having a blast.

SARA: Good for Chris.

JOSH: But Chris is a real people person. We were at school together.

SARA: Oh, one of those. God save us from people persons. Or is the plural of people person, people people?

JOSH: Oh. I think…

SARA: Don't you think twenty four is a bit young to be getting married?

JOSH: We're twenty four.

SARA: Exactly.

Beat.

JOSH: I've got to make the best man speech in a sec.

SARA: Oh shit, really? That'll be a barrel of laughs. Sorry, I'm a bit drunk.

JOSH: Right. I've written some decent jokes, actually.

SARA: Jokes? This sounds worse than I thought.

JOSH: I'm hurt by that remark. Frankly.

SARA: Better let me read it, give you the benefit of my expertise. Writing is my *trade.*

JOSH: (*Beat. JOSH pulls out the speech and gives it to SARA.*) When you say 'your *trade*', you mean your job at that local rag, is that correct?

SARA: (*Reading.*) Mm? It's a start.

JOSH: (*Pause.*) Well?

SARA: You don't really believe all this crap, do you?

JOSH: What crap?

SARA: All this dreary slop about your one true soul-mate. See this is why I hate weddings. It brings out the American in everyone.

JOSH: You have to say that stuff.

SARA: Is that how you feel about The Lovely Melanie?

JOSH: Could you stop calling her The Lovely Melanie?

SARA: Why? Isn't she?

JOSH: No. Yes. She's all right.

SARA: 'All right?' Wow. Don't hyperventilate with enthusiasm Josh. Jesus.

JOSH: (*Beat.*) Are you… (*Grins.*)

SARA: What?

JOSH: You're not… (*Grins.*)

SARA: Will you stop *grinning* like that, it's horrid.

JOSH: Are you jealous?

Beat.

SARA: I beg your pardon.

JOSH: Of Melanie?

SARA: You should put that in your speech, it's the best joke of the lot. It's hysterical.

JOSH: Seriously.

SARA: Shut up. Jealous?

JOSH: Are you?

He is very close. They hold a tense look.

SARA: What if I am? A tiny bit.

JOSH smiles. Beat.

JOSH: I have to make my speech now.

JOSH goes off. SARA watches him.

SARA: (*To herself.*) Good luck.

SAM returns.

SAM: Just wanted to wash my hands, but I couldn't get the soap out.

SARA: (*Distracted.*) Hmm?

SAM: I kept bashing my fist down on the little knob, there's nothing coming out.

SARA: Dad…

SAM: They can't just have a tap you twist?

SARA: I'm going back to Jerusalem.

SAM: (*Beat.*) Oh. That's quick.

SARA: I want to do a story about…

SAM: It's a very tense time.

SARA: Yes. I know.

SAM: Raving lunatics blowing themselves up all over the place.

SARA: …don't start this…

SAM: …families out for a meal, doing the shopping…

SARA: …yes…

SAM: …getting blown apart…

SARA: Are you having a dessert?

SAM: It's no wonder the Israelis are coming down hard. It's the only language the Arabs understand.

SARA: (*Reading the menu.*) OK. Let's see.

SAM: We've tried the other way. We've tried talking. We offered them a deal at Camp David and they spat it back on our faces.

SARA: Oh look, they've got lemon tart.

SAM: I know you think everyone should get along and hold hands, but the truth is…

SARA: It comes with crème fraiche.

SAM: The truth is…everyone hates Jews. It's not news to me. I grew up in the East End with Mosley's thugs.

SARA: You like crème fraiche.

SAM: Black shirts beating up old women, kids…just because they were Jews.

SARA: They'll probably put a dollop on the side or something.

SAM: And it's still going on. Jewish graves smashed and vandalised…

SARA: All minorities get attacked. Shit happens. But it doesn't mean we should all pack our bags and move to Israel.

SAM: Other people aren't my concern. *My* people are my concern.

SARA: But everyone should be your concern. That's what I'm saying…

SAM: You think you got a choice about this?

SARA: I see things differently to you. I always have.

SAM: No. You got no choice. You're Jewish in your DNA. It's written in your hair, in your eyes, in your skin, in your soul.

SARA: I have to be able to criticise. To ask more of people… I…

SAM: God gave us the bible Sara. The Ten Commandments, the law. He didn't give it to the Turks or – or the *Belgians*, he gave it to us.

SARA: Don't you sometimes wish he had given it to the Belgians? Let them have all this crap. God knows they deserve it.

SAM: When you attack Israel, you attack me.

SARA: We forgive, over and over, we forgive brutality because it's all in the name of –

SAM: Yes, because it's kill or be killed. That's…

SARA: That's really what you believe?

SAM: Yes. It's really what I believe. And I believe that while we're better at killing them than they are at killing us, we have a chance.

SARA: This is wrong. How can you not see that? Killing innocent people is just wrong. Under any circumstance. It has to be, otherwise we're lost.

SAM: Sara, I'm telling you as your father. You've got to stop writing those articles.

SARA: You're *telling* me?

SAM: Yes. I'm *telling* you. Write about something else. Pick another subject. There's plenty of conflict, plenty of people doing dodgy things. Why this? Why d'you have to write about this?

SARA: The Middle East…it's the vortex. It's where it's happening. In Israel, the line's been drawn in the sand and it demands scrutiny. And it's *my* field. I'm just beginning to get to grips with it.

SAM: Don't you understand? What you're doing disgusts me.

SARA: … Dad…

SAM: You're a traitor. A traitor to your own people.

Long pause.

Is it…are you bitter? Is that it?

SARA: Bitter?

SAM: Because you don't have a man? Has it made you bitter? Is that where it all went wrong with you?

SARA: *What?*

SAM: Maybe it's my fault. Did I fail you in some way? Maybe I didn't bring you up right. Maybe that's why you're still single.

SARA: … I'm gonna scream…

SAM: Let me take you shopping, get you a nice top.

SARA: (*Exploding.*) I don't want a nice top! I'm not a child! Christ, I'm nearly forty!

Silence. The WAITER arrives.

Just the bill please.

WAITER nods and goes. Pause. SARA stares at SAM wanting to speak. Finally…

You've got to let me go.

WAITER arrives with the bill. He hovers by SAM, but SAM gestures to give it to SARA.

(*Still looking at SAM.*) Thanks.

Darkness.

Scene 3

JOSH's cell.

OFFICER: Are you ready to talk?

JOSH: (*Nothing.*)

OFFICER: You had captured a man breaking the curfew.

Lighting change. We are on a dust road on the West Bank. A man – YUSEF – enters and falls to his knees. JOSH starts to tie his hands behind his back.

JOSH: (*As he ties.*) For the last time…shut up! Shut up!

YUSEF: I didn't say anything.

JOSH: Don't talk back. Understand?

JOSH finishes binding YUSEF's hands and stands up.

Understand?

JOSH picks up his M-16 and aims it at the man's head.

YUSEF: You told me not to speak.

JOSH whacks him over the head with the butt of his gun.

JOSH: Shut it!

YUSEF moans and falls over.

Get up.

YUSEF tries to scramble to his feet.

On your knees. What did I say?

YUSEF: You said get up.

JOSH whacks YUSEF over the head.

JOSH: I said no talking. Are you thick?

YUSEF: Can you stop hitting me please?

JOSH: Stop disobeying me and I'll stop hitting you. It's simple logic.

YUSEF: You're trapping me with it.

JOSH: Explain to me why this is so difficult.

YUSEF: I can't… I can't win with you.

JOSH: Explain why it is so difficult for you to shut the fuck up?

YUSEF: I'm trying to do what you want.

JOSH whacks YUSEF again.

Please.

JOSH: This is the only thing you understand isn't it?

YUSEF: No. I don't understand it at all. It just hurts.

JOSH hits him again.

Stop doing that.

JOSH: Wanker.

YUSEF: I just wanted to buy a newspaper.

JOSH: You broke the curfew.

YUSEF: My father wanted to read the news.

JOSH: You mustn't break the curfew.

YUSEF: My father's very demanding.

JOSH: The curfew is there for a reason.

YUSEF: You don't have my father.

JOSH: Do you understand? The curfew!

YUSEF: He won't settle until he has his paper.

JOSH: You do not break the curfew. Not for anything.

YUSEF: He likes to keep abreast of the news.

JOSH: Please. Please. Just – please – don't fuck with me, all right, don't fuck with me today. I haven't slept for four days. There's been a dogfight in Tulkarem, I've been separated from my unit, so don't – I mean what? What, you think I want this? Standing in this fucking hovel whiling away the time with you?

YUSEF: Then let me go home.

JOSH: It's not what I'd choose to do, believe me.

YUSEF: All right, so let me go home.

JOSH: Home?

YUSEF: It's just over there.

JOSH: You walk over there, you'll get shot.

YUSEF: I'll take my chances.

JOSH: Are you stupid or what? I just told you…

YUSEF: It's better than staying here with you to be cracked over the top of the head.

JOSH: I am trying to protect you. Don't you get it?

YUSEF: I have to admit I'm struggling with the logic.

JOSH hits him.

Ah! Why did you hit me?

JOSH: Sorry. Reflex reaction. You were saying?

YUSEF: Let me go home.

JOSH: Home? I can't go home.

YUSEF: I'm truly sorry to hear that.

JOSH: I have to stay here until....

YUSEF: Until?

JOSH gets out a piece of rag.

What are you doing?

JOSH ties the rag around YUSEF's eyes.

Ah no.

JOSH: Quiet.

YUSEF: Please.

JOSH: If you lot didn't insist on blowing up children on buses I wouldn't have to be here. All right?

YUSEF: Yes. I'm sorry about that. It's a little fetish we Palestinians have. We like to blow up children.

JOSH: Are you being cute?

YUSEF: You know the English like their tea and crumpets. It's just a thing.

JOSH: You've got a fucking nerve.

YUSEF: The Greeks like to smash plates. We like to blow up Jewish children.

JOSH: You think this is something to joke about?

YUSEF: When you're in my position you're a joker or a killer. Believe me. Jokers are better.

JOSH's radio starts to burble.

JOSH: Shalom! (*The radio burbles.*) When are you coming? (*Burble.*) Yes, yes, I'll wait here. But you'll be here soon. (*Burble.*) I don't know what happened to them we got separated. (*Burble.*) Come on, I'm on my own, here, I need… I can't…but I can't. (*Burble.*) OK, but I caught… (*Burble.*) Yes, but I caught… (*Burble.*) OK. Bye.

Pause. JOSH sits, thinking intensely.

There was a Rabbi, a Priest and an Iman…

YUSEF: What are you doing?

JOSH: You think Jews can't tell jokes?

YUSEF: You're telling me a joke?

JOSH: I learnt this where I grew up.

YUSEF: You're doing comedy now?

JOSH: That's right. Jews invented it.

YUSEF: All right. Get on with it.

JOSH: (*Beat.*) I've forgotten it now.

YUSEF: Brilliant.

JOSH: I'm not a great joke teller, all right?

YUSEF: Some Jew you are.

JOSH: Shut up.

YUSEF: Please. Don't hit me again.

JOSH: Fuck.

YUSEF: Why is there so much hate in you?

JOSH: My friend died here. OK? Right here.

YUSEF: People die here. My uncle had olive groves. The Israelis came and tore up the whole place for no reason. His whole livelihood. He stood in front of the bulldozers to stop them. Generations had looked after these olive groves, the whole history of his family. He stood in front of the bulldozers. But they didn't stop. They kept on going. The rolled over him.

JOSH: My friend was on his way home when he took the wrong road. He was jumped by a group. They doused him with petrol and set him on fire while he was still alive. His girlfriend rang him on his pellephone and one of the group answered. The guy who answered the phone told her in Hebrew, 'You'll never see your boyfriend again'. (*Beat.*) I held his sister in my arms as she sobbed and begged me to promise her that he didn't feel any pain. How could I do that and look her in the eyes? I couldn't. (*Pause.*) You people. You…animals. What do you expect from us? How do you expect to be treated? I mean we have…we are…we have one of the best classical orchestras in the world. Zubin Mehta directs it. What do you have? You animals.

Pause.

YUSEF: What are you going to do to me?

JOSH: I have to wait for orders.

YUSEF: I just wanted to get a paper, I…

JOSH: I have to wait for orders. That's it.

Pause.

YUSEF: So where did you grow up?

JOSH: What?

YUSEF: You said you learnt that joke where you grew up.

JOSH: Don't try and make chit chat with me.

YUSEF: Come on. Tell me. We're stuck here for who knows how long.

JOSH: St John's Wood.

YUSEF: Sinjin's wood?

JOSH: It's in London.

YUSEF: You're English?

JOSH: Not anymore.

YUSEF: What's it like in Sinjin's Wood?

Beat.

JOSH: Full of Arabs.

Pause.

OFFICER: You know, I don't understand it. Compared to the combat situations you've been in, this was nothing. And I read you were engaged in a knife fight with an enemy combatant in Jenin. You survived it, uninjured. You held him prisoner. You're tough.

JOSH: You can't treat me like this.

OFFICER: For an English boy, I mean.

JOSH: I'm a citizen. I'm an Israeli.

OFFICER: At the moment you're a prisoner.

JOSH: What do you want? You know what happened.

OFFICER: Yes.

JOSH: So what more do you want from me?

OFFICER: Tell me about the story. The one about your father.

JOSH: Why? What's that got to do with all this?

OFFICER: You tell me.

JOSH: What?

OFFICER: Tell me why you wrote the story?

JOSH: I can't answer that.

OFFICER: Try.

JOSH: My father…it's his story I just…

OFFICER: Your father didn't approve of you making *aliyah*?

JOSH: No.

OFFICER: He was an anti-Zionist.

JOSH: Yes. No. Yes.

OFFICER: He publicly attacked Israel on television. In the newspaper…

JOSH: I'm not my father.

OFFICER: And yet you write his story. You publish his words.

JOSH: My words.

OFFICER: OK.

OFFICER takes out a book.

JOSH: You going to read me a bedtime story?

OFFICER: You see it seems to me, and I'm no professor, but it seems to me, this is a story about a Jew who turns against his people. And yet you don't condemn him.

JOSH: (*Slowly. Quietly.*) I'm an Israeli.

OFFICER: Let's talk some more about your father.

Darkness.

ACT TWO

Scene 1

MAX's room. SAM stands at the doorway with YASMIN.

YASMIN: He's just with the doctor. He won't be long.

SAM: Thanks.

YASMIN: There's some water on the side there if you're thirsty.

SAM nods. YASMIN goes. Silence. SAM goes over to the side table and starts to pour himself a glass of water.

Lights change. Enter JOSH. SAM speaks without looking up.

SAM: Can I get you a drink, Josh?

JOSH: Thanks.

SAM: Whiskey?

JOSH: Whiskey would be great.

SAM: Good for you.

SAM pours two whiskeys.

How's your Mum?

JOSH: She's got a date.

SAM: A date? People of our age don't date.

JOSH: Sheldon.

SAM: What about that, a date?

JOSH: It's good she's moving on.

SAM: And you're thinking of moving to Israel, I hear.

JOSH: Yes. Mr Levy… I wanted to…

SAM: Call me Sam.

JOSH: Right. I wanted to…

SAM: That's a wonderful thing to make *aliyah.* To live in a country of Jews. An amazing thought.

JOSH: Yes. I'm twenty five now, and I feel I should…

SAM: Jewish policemen. Jewish postmen. Jewish plumbers. Jewish bus drivers. Jewish neighbours. Jewish lumberjacks. Do they have lumberjacks in Israel?

JOSH: I can check it out for you if you like.

SAM: Thanks. And you think… I mean after this handshake.

JOSH: The White House Lawn?

SAM: Did you see it? We've got CNN. I had it installed. We got a dish on the side of the house.

JOSH: I saw the dish.

SAM: Oh yes it's very high tech. Very space age. We watched that handshake all day. They had it on a loop. I never got bored.

JOSH: I think Sara's watching CNN.

SAM: She's glued to the news now.

JOSH: Yeah.

SAM: I mean they gave them all Nobel Peace Prizes, that's got to mean something…the Nobel Peace Prize.

JOSH: Mr Levy… I wanted to ask…

SAM: Oh. Your whiskey. I forgot. (*Gives JOSH a glass.*)

JOSH: Thanks.

SAM: You were saying?

JOSH: Sara and I have been together…we've been going out for nearly a year…

SAM: Yes.

JOSH: …and I wanted to ask…you know…for your… permission…or at least your blessing.

SAM: Oh.

JOSH: I know it's a bit…old fashioned.

SAM: No. No. Well, yes. But.

JOSH: I want to marry her.

SAM: And you'd still be moving to Israel?

JOSH: I haven't spoken to Sara yet. I'm going to do it tonight. After dinner.

SAM: Sara? Sara's going too?

JOSH: Well yes. I mean if we're married…

SAM: So you'd both be living in Israel?

JOSH: That's the plan.

SAM: Right. Of course. I didn't think it through.

JOSH: Right.

SAM: No. It's a wonderful thing…but I mean…you know…won't you miss your family? Your friends?

JOSH: They'll visit. Even Chris said he'd come.

SAM: Chris?

JOSH: From school. He was at the wedding last year.

SAM: Was he?

JOSH: Yes. You remember he won the prize for dancing the best *horra.*

SAM: A bloke called Chris won the prize for dancing the best *horra*? What is he, Church of England?

JOSH: I don't think he goes to church.

SAM: No. Right. (*Beat.*) What did he win? For dancing the best…

JOSH: Yes.

SAM: Did he win something?

JOSH: Socks.

SAM: Socks? Who gives socks?

JOSH: They had Fred Flintstone on them.

SAM: The cartoon character?

JOSH: Yeah.

SAM: What about that?

JOSH: Mr Levy. Sara will be OK. Safe I mean.

SAM: Yeah. Of course. I mean they shook hands didn't they? On the White House Lawn.

SARA comes in looking flustered and disturbed. She stands there for a moment.

JOSH: What is it?

SARA: Rabin's been shot.

JOSH follows SARA out. SAM stares ahead. Lights change back. Enter MAX.

MAX: Oh. It's you. Whoop de do.

MAX goes and sits on his bed. He is a little out of breath.

SAM: So how you doing?

MAX: They've given me three months to live.

SAM: Right. I heard. Long as it's nothing serious.

MAX: Hmm.

Pause. MAX beckons SAM over and whispers.

I'll tell you something. They're trying to do me in faster though.

SAM: What?

MAX: They want me gone. They need the beds you see, so they're trying to kill me off quick. Get it over with.

SAM: It's all right, you can complain to me. I'm your agent, that's what my ten per cent's for.

MAX: You think I'm joking?

SAM: How are they going to kill you off?

MAX: Right. Listen to this one. They told me I had a build up of fluid in my legs. Told me I wouldn't be able to walk by myself again. Last Tuesday they told me this. All right so this morning I leapt out of bed and went for a Jimmy Riddle like I was twenty two. So this doctor just now, this schoolboy, this twelve year old, he says: he no longer believes there's fluid in my legs. That he believes there's some other problem. 'What other problem?' I say. 'Give it a name. Make me feel better if my pain's got a name.' Says he doesn't know what it is, just it isn't fluid in my legs.

SAM: So what are you saying? They're trying to confuse you to death?

MAX: I cried the other day. Actual tears. At the thought of how quick it all goes. How fragile it all is. Life. It slips through your fingers like confetti on a breezy day.

SAM: When I go I think I'll be grateful for the rest.

MAX: You won't be alone there.

SAM: Thanks.

MAX: And how much I forget. The little things. I got a memory of things in my bones. A feeling about people and…but I can't see faces. Don't know names.

SAM: Have you prayed?

MAX: Don't be a *schmarel.* What am I gonna pray for? When you're dead, you're dead.

SAM: You're like the Jewish horse who walks into a bar. The barman says, 'Why the long face?' The horse says, 'What have I got to be happy about, I'm a horse.'

MAX: You've been telling that joke for forty years and it's never been funny.

SAM: Here's another one.

MAX: Don't you have anything better to do than annoy me?

SAM: This one is germane to the point.

MAX: I should have sacked you years ago. I could have gone with Curtis Brown.

SAM: So Solly meets Morty in the street.

MAX: Gelberg was begging me.

SAM: And Morty's in a right state.

MAX: He was on his knees, Gelberg.

SAM: He says, 'Solly, I've got terrible problems. I've got to pay ten thousand pounds in two weeks.' 'So? Easy,' says Solly. 'Just get ten thousand candles and sell them each for a pound.' And Morty says 'But I don't have any candles.' And Solly says, 'No candles you say? Then you've got problems.' It's the same with you. You've got no religion. No fall back position. You've got no candles.

MAX: You're a first class potz. You know that? (*Beat.*) My son came to see me. He's back from Israel.

SAM: I sometimes wonder if the babies got swapped. That you should be Sara's Dad and I should be Josh's.

MAX: Sara's a brave girl.

SAM: My luck to have a brave daughter. She can't be terrified like everyone else?

MAX: I never see Josh. He never calls. All I do is worry.

SAM: He has something to fight for. He's defending the homeland.

MAX: He's a fanatic. He gets it from his mother.

SAM: Young men are passionate. We were passionate. We marched against the fascists when we were young. We took to the streets, didn't we?

MAX: We had a just cause.

SAM: But the passion was the thing. Not the cause, just to be young and passionate. To *feel*...you know...to *feel*...but...you know, you get less certain with age.

Pause.

So Sandra sends her love.

MAX: Oh yeah?

SAM: Says she'll make you some soup.

MAX: That's nice.

SAM: Isn't it?

MAX: Very. (*Beat.*) So who's Sandra?

SAM: What?

MAX: Who's Sandra?

SAM: Who's Sandra?

MAX: Do I know her?

SAM: What? She's my wife!

MAX: Your wife?!

SAM: How long have you known me? Fifty years. Sixty?

MAX: What happened to the other one?

SAM: What other one?

MAX: What happened to Susan?

SAM: Who the hell is Susan?

MAX: Susan. Susan. Your wife. Don't you know your own wife?

SAM: My wife's name is Sandra.

MAX: Sandra?

SAM: We've been married for thirty eight years. How can you get that wrong?

MAX: You're absolutely right. It's Sandra. Not Susan.

SAM: I KNOW THAT!

MAX: All right, don't shout.

SAM: She's fine. Sandra's fine. Not sleeping at night.

MAX: Why not? You doing the nudging?

SAM: Yeah, well…that and the man next door who coughs.

MAX: What man who coughs?

SAM: Next door. He's got this hacking cough. Keeps us up half the night.

MAX: Sounds like he smokes too much.

SAM: He does it on purpose. He's an anti-Semite.

MAX: Because he coughs?

SAM: There's a particular tone to his cough.

MAX: You think people don't wheeze all bloody night round here? What, are they all anti-Semites?

SAM: Maybe. I don't know them do I? I don't know their affiliations.

MAX: Look, I've got a few good months left, I don't want to fill them with this foolishness.

SAM: I mean he puts up pictures…at Easter time…he puts up large posters of Jesus.

MAX: Get me Gelberg on the phone. Get him on the phone.

SAM: Posters of yoshki on the cross, arms out-stretched, the whole bit. Like to say, you, you lot did this. You bastards.

MAX: Come on.

SAM: And you're telling me he's not a Jew hater?

MAX: No. I don't think he's a Jew hater, Sammy, I think he's a You hater. There's a difference. You've got a talent for aggravating people. You always have.

SAM: I'm nothing but civil to the man. I breathe, he's unhappy.

MAX: You're paranoid. I blame your parents.

SAM: Yeah. When I was a kid they didn't like me to tell people I was Jewish. They were scared. They said if anyone asks your religion, tell them you're Greek Orthodox.

MAX: I remember. You got beaten up by a gang of Turkish kids.

SAM: That's true.

MAX laughs. SAM joins in. Eventually the laughter dies.

I don't mind telling you, I'm going to miss you when you go. You've made me a lot of money.

MAX: Funny you should say that. (*MAX pulls the pages from under his pillow.*) Because I haven't finished yet.

SAM: Max. You've been working. That's terrific. Let me see. (*SAM takes the pages and looks over them. MAX watches him intently.*) Yes. Hmm. That's good. Uh-huh. Uh-huh.

MAX: Don't make the noises, just read it.

SAM reads on. Suddenly he starts to frown.

SAM: No!

He turns the pages anxiously. Then he starts to scan the rest of the story frantically. Then he slams the pages down and stands up, more furious now than we've seen him.

No, no, no, no, no.

MAX: A structure problem perhaps?

SAM: You think this is funny?

MAX: I'm just telling a story, Sammy.

SAM: How could you write about this? It's gone, forgotten.

MAX: Not for me.

SAM: Why would you want to do that to me? To us? Why would you want to dredge up all that business?

MAX: I want you to publish this when I'm dead.

SAM: What's past is past.

MAX: The past is all I have now. My life is in those pages!

SAM: No. No. I'm not doing it. I won't let you write about Weinstein.

MAX: Sammy. This is my past.

SAM: Our past. You have no right. No right!

MAX: I want this published.

SAM: I'm not talking to you about this.

MAX: We will have this conversation if it's the last one I have, Sam.

SAM: What happened with Weinstein, what we did, it's… (over)

MAX: …it's a disgrace. We have to face what we did.

SAM: We did nothing to be ashamed of. We did what had to be done. Your words.

MAX: We beat him and kicked him and…

SAM: 'Let's string him up,' you said. 'Come on lads, let's teach Weinstein a lesson he'll never forget!'

MAX: We crucified him!

SAM: Don't exaggerate.

MAX: We stripped him and tied him to a cross!

SAM: A tree! And we didn't bang nails into his hands and feet, don't get all Wagnerian about it. You writers. Always making something out of nothing.

MAX: If it's nothing, why you getting all jittery about it?

SAM: Because it's over. Weinstein tried to join the fascist party. Tried to give them names and addresses so they fire-bomb people's homes. Jewish homes. Right, so we taught him a lesson and no-one ever heard from him again. End of story.

MAX: And that's another thing… What about what happened afterwards?

SAM: Max…

MAX: Because somebody must have been watching us.

SAM: Right. And in the last God-knows-how-many years since it's been, has anyone come forward?

MAX: That's not the point and you know it.

SAM: Has anyone mentioned it?

MAX: Somebody must have seen us that night.

SAM: Nobody saw.

MAX: Somebody removed Weinstein from that cross.

SAM: That doesn't mean anything.

MAX: He vanished. He was gone. The next morning there was a hunk of wood and some ropes and no Weinstein.

SAM: OK.

MAX: He didn't disappear of his own accord did he?

SAM: Max…

MAX: The skies didn't open and send a bolt of…an…an angel didn't descend from the heavens and swoop up Weinstein…there was no miracle!

SAM: How do you know?

Beat. MAX throws his hands in the air.

MAX: I don't.

SAM: You see…anything's possible.

MAX: Sam…

SAM: Why is it so important to you? Why this? Why now?

MAX: Because it affects everything. Everything we do in our lives has a consequence. The chickens always come home to roost.

SAM: I don't know what you mean.

MAX: Look at Josh. He's making the same mistakes we did.

SAM: This is about Josh?

MAX: I have to put this right before it's too late.

SAM: Not now. Not now. Now I have to go. I have to…

MAX: Sammy.

SAM: Susan's making dinner. I have to go.

SAM turns to leave. MAX suddenly remembers and points his finger wildly.

MAX: Sandra!

SAM: What?

MAX: You mean Sandra's making dinner!

SAM: What did I say?

MAX: You said Susan's making dinner!

SAM: No. Sandra. My wife's name is Sandra.

MAX: Right. Susan's the other one.

SAM stares. Darkness.

Scene 2

YASMIN's flat. TARIQ enters with a carrier bag full of food.

TARIQ: There's salad, pita, humus…

YASMIN: You're always buying me stuff.

TARIQ: I got lamb as well.

YASMIN: Halal. Of course.

TARIQ: Dad said you weren't eating properly.

YASMIN: Dad's the one who doesn't eat properly.

TARIQ: He just eats that Happy Burger muck all the time.

YASMIN: It's called Planet Burger and I have to go.

TARIQ: When will you be back?

YASMIN: I don't know. I'm late.

TARIQ: Yas.

YASMIN: I don't have to answer to you.

TARIQ: I'm your brother.

YASMIN: Yeah, not my father.

TARIQ: Dad's no good at this. He lets you do what you want. He's weak.

YASMIN: Leave him alone.

TARIQ: Come on Yas, what does he look like in that joker's costume?

YASMIN: That's his uniform.

TARIQ: He looks like a clown.

YASMIN: He's proud of it.

TARIQ: I know he is. That's what makes me want to chuck up.

YASMIN: He has to work. He can't stand not working.

TARIQ: … It's not a job for a man…clearing shit after a bunch of chav kids. You know they call him Spakie Pakie, have you heard them? And he fucking smiles. He fucking grins at them. It makes me want to take a torch to that place.

YASMIN: I have to go. Thanks for the stuff.

TARIQ: When will you be back?

YASMIN: There isn't a curfew, this is England

TARIQ: I know that. When will you be back?

YASMIN: Goodbye Tariq.

He stops her.

TARIQ: You can't be trusted.

YASMIN: Get off me.

TARIQ: You're lacking in modesty.

YASMIN: God, you've really lost it with this religious crap.

TARIQ: I'm the only one in the family with morality.

YASMIN: Jesus you sound like one of those…

TARIQ: You're lost. You don't have God.

YASMIN: Get out of my way please Tariq.

TARIQ: You speak to me like that and I'll bloody beat you until you understand!

Beat. YASMIN is a little taken aback by TARIQ's force.

No, listen to me. No, because…I know where I am. Where I come from. What my destiny is.

YASMIN: OK. OK fine. Let me know how that goes for you…

She tries to go again and he stops her, more forcefully this time.

TARIQ: I believe. I have Allah. What do you have? Nothing.

YASMIN: I'm a nurse. Today I had to wipe some old woman's bleeding arse, so don't tell me I'm lost.

TARIQ: Is that the woman who wouldn't let you touch her, because you were – what was it? A muslim bitch.

YASMIN: She has bowel cancer. It took all we had just to make her comfortable.

TARIQ: Didn't she spit in your face when you tried to help her?

YASMIN: That was someone else and it's not usually like that…it doesn't happen a lot.

TARIQ: You're the sick person. Until you accept Allah into your heart you're as sick as they are. Sick in your soul.

YASMIN: I have to go out.

TARIQ: For a shag?

YASMIN: Whatever. Yeah. Whatever. I'm gonna shag some bloke, is that what you want to hear?

TARIQ: At home you wouldn't get away with behaving like this.

YASMIN: At home?

TARIQ: In Pakistan.

YASMIN: We're from Leicester!

TARIQ: Wake up Yas. They don't want us here. That's why you have to be like me. I care about my God. I care about my brothers. I care about my nation.

YASMIN: What about me? Do you care about me?

TARIQ: What? Yeah. I…I care you're not an English slapper innit.

YASMIN: I'm not going out for a shag, OK? I was only winding you up.

Loaded pause.

TARIQ: What about Brian then?

Silence. YASMIN looks at him furious and surprised.

YASMIN: What?

TARIQ: Someone's got to look out for you.

YASMIN: You followed me?

TARIQ: Sort of. So?

YASMIN: You wanker.

TARIQ: He's the wanker. He lives with his fucking mum innit.

YASMIN: I don't believe this.

TARIQ: He wanted to use you. To tell all his mates how he had a bit of Asian pussy. Because that kind of guy, he don't care about nothing.

YASMIN: Stay out of my life! I don't need you to protect me.

TARIQ: You think we're all safe and British but they got people. Working away. Planning. This is not our country.

YASMIN: We're as British as anyone. Look around.

TARIQ: Fuck Britain. I got nothing in common with these people innit. All they do is drink and fight and throw up and fall over. Their lives have no value, you know? They only care about buying a bigger car, a bigger house, they look at people with more than them and they feel small.

YASMIN: You used to be normal. What is this shit you're talking? I don't understand it.

TARIQ: The Prophet – peace be upon him – said: 'Give the son of Adam a mountain of gold and he'll want another one'. So we have to change the world. By force. Show them. Change or die. (*YASMIN is shaking her head, on the verge of tears.*) This is our destiny. This is Allah's fury. It's been coming and it's unstoppable. (*Chanting and pounding his fist.*) Me against my brother! Me and my brother against our cousins! Me, my brother and my cousins against the world!

YASMIN: Tariq…

TARIQ: Don't go out tonight.

YASMIN: It scares me when you talk like that.

TARIQ: If you shag that Brian geezer…

YASMIN: Please Tariq.

TARIQ: I swear to you.

YASMIN: Then what? You'll what?

TARIQ: You'll bring shame on your family.

YASMIN: OK, that's enough…

TARIQ: If you go…

YASMIN: You'll what?

TARIQ: If you go. Like a whore!

YASMIN: Yes? If I go…if I'm a whore…then what? Then I'm a whore. And what?

TARIQ: If…if…if you…

YASMIN: Then what? Then what?

TARIQ: Then I'll punish you.

YASMIN: Goodbye Tariq.

YASMIN tries again to leave, but TARIQ stands in her way.

TARIQ: You're not going anywhere. (*YASMIN shakes.*) Now. (*Pointing wildly at the bag of food.*) Make me dinner, woman.

Beat.

YASMIN: Fuck you.

TARIQ: You'll regret that.

YASMIN pushes past TARIQ.

You'll regret that. (*Shouting after her violently.*) YASMIN! I'll make you regret that!!

Darkness.

Scene 3

Bar.

JOSH and SARA are drinking at a table.

SARA: So.

JOSH: So.

SARA: Look at you.

JOSH: What?

SARA: Life out there agrees with you, Joshua.

JOSH: Yeah?

SARA: Yeah, you look really…you know, you're tanned and…quite big.

JOSH: Well, I'm out in the desert aren't I? I mean…

SARA: No, seriously you look really…

JOSH: Oh and I mean you…you look…

SARA: Oh, too late.

JOSH: No, come on, you look great.

SARA: Too late, too late.

JOSH: You know I'm no good at that kind of thing. Compliments.

SARA: You're a nightmare.

JOSH: True.

SARA: So is there anyone…any…young lady?

JOSH: No. There was. Not just now. It's been…you know…

SARA: Yeah.

JOSH: But I bet you've…you know…

SARA: What?

JOSH: Well…

SARA: Are you being…

JOSH: No, I bet you've had a few since…

SARA: Are you calling me a slapper?

JOSH: No, but…I know you Sara. I know you better than you know yourself.

SARA: Well. No. I don't think you do.

Beat.

JOSH: Well…It's been a long time.

SARA: Six years.

JOSH: Makes me feel old.

SARA: Well you are thirty two, no spring chicken.

JOSH: What?

SARA: Nothing. I do miss you.

JOSH: Yeah?

Beat.

SARA: How's your Dad?

JOSH: Dying. How's yours?

SARA: Disapproving.

JOSH: I don't know what's more difficult.

SARA: I just had supper with him. It wasn't easy.

Pause.

JOSH: So, I read some of your articles.

SARA: Do you mind if we don't do this now?

JOSH: I don't mind telling you, you've disappointed me.

SARA: Oh really? Well…

JOSH: I mean now we're not together, we can be honest with each other. Right?

SARA: So we should lie to each other if we're together, is that what you're saying?

JOSH: No. Lying was *your* little vice when we were going out.

Beat. SARA is contrite.

SARA: Listen, I…write what… I'm doing my job. I won't apologise for…

JOSH: How do you presume to judge Israel?

SARA: Josh…

JOSH: Are you there? Do you live there? Are you standing up to be counted?

SARA: Can't we change the subject? I haven't seen you in years. Can't we talk about something else?

JOSH: NO! We can't change the subject! This is the subject! There is no other subject. Not for us.

SARA: Josh…

JOSH: Not when this morning eighteen kids were blown apart by another suicide bomber. Just this morning. Some of them clinging to each other as they fried.

SARA: Yes.

JOSH: How do you negotiate with this? How? How? How do you sit down with people who are prepared to do this? Do they really think they're going to paradise? Is this the key to eternal happiness? Killing children? Shooting pregnant women in the stomach? Is this their culture? Their religion? We don't want to be in the West Bank, we don't want war, but please, I'm asking you, give us an alternative.

SARA: After the bombing in Megiddo Junction the leader of Islamic Jihad said, 'To those who tell us to stop the Martyrdom operations we say: give us an alternative'. The very same words.

JOSH: Sara…

SARA: In two years as a correspondent out there, I haven't come across a single Palestinian who hasn't lost a son or daughter, husband, father, brother, sister, lover…

JOSH: How can you sympathise with these people? This is pure evil. Pure hate. They pack shards of glass and nails into their bombs so if they don't kill outright, they at least maim. Cripple. Blind. Men, women, children. This is the utter slime that crawls across the earth. These are worms, vile, vile, vile – we must never, never, never tolerate this. No. They must be stopped. And we'll stop them with the only thing they understand. Force.

SARA: Force? On a people locked inside a fence, suffering from acute malnutrition? On a people with no army, no airforce, no state, no jobs, no hospitals, no sewage? Whose government buildings are destroyed? Whose roads between cities are inaccessible to them? Force? On a people who have no rights and no hope.

Beat.

JOSH: You used to believe Sara. You used to believe in Israel. We started from the same place. How did we come so far apart?

SARA: I don't know. I don't know. But I think… I think that day…the day Rabin was killed. Shot by a settler. A Jew. I suddenly thought… We're just like everyone else. Not special. Not chosen. We don't think with one mind. We're fractured, we're confused and if we go on like we are, we're finished. (*Pause.*) Josh, I have to go. I have to meet someone.

JOSH: Oh. OK. Got a date?

SARA: Actually yes.

SARA stands up. Beat.

SARA: When we were going out I did a horrible thing to you. I'm sorry about that.

JOSH: I always envied you.

SARA: Why?

JOSH: Your parents were so…

SARA: I don't…

JOSH: My Dad never…the whole Jewish thing. We never dealt with it. When I was a kid… I mean I knew I was Jewish, I knew, I mean I *felt*…different. I just didn't know why. And Dad said to forget about it, that we were all human beings and that's the end of it. I had these two friends…we were twelve…we did everything together. When they found out I was Jewish they told me they couldn't be my friend anymore. I said why? They said because I killed Jesus. I said, I don't know what you're talking about, I didn't do anything. They said the Jews are responsible. The Jews had to pay. Something in me… I don't know what it was, but something rose in me. This rage. I fought them. Then when I got home, I tried to write a story about it. I…and…

SARA: And?

JOSH: I'm… I don't know what it is, but I've had this feeling for a long time. A really long time. I'm incredibly angry. All the time. Just extremely angry.

SARA: Yeah. I should…

JOSH: Sure. Have a good time on your date.

Beat. SARA goes. JOSH carries on drinking when YASMIN enters from the toilets carrying a gin and tonic.

Funny.

YASMIN: What is?

JOSH: Bumping into you here.

YASMIN: Hysterical.

JOSH: I was just meeting an old friend.

YASMIN: Right.

JOSH: We met here for a drink.

YASMIN: It's OK, I didn't think you were stalking me.

JOSH: God, of course not. Not that you… I mean I'm not saying you wouldn't be the kind of person I'd stalk. (*Beat.*) If I was inclined to…stalk…someone. Um. Are you here on your own?

YASMIN: (*Puts down her drink and sits.*) I think I've been blown out.

JOSH: By whom?

YASMIN: This guy. Brian. I was supposed to meet him forty-five minutes ago. This is my fourth gin and tonic.

JOSH: What's that, about one every ten minutes?

YASMIN stares at JOSH.

I'm sorry, I didn't know what to say.

YASMIN: Don't feel you have to say something.

JOSH: Right.

YASMIN: I think my brother scared him off.

JOSH: Oh?

YASMIN: He likes to stick his nose in where he's not wanted and impose his particular lunacy on everyone else.

JOSH: It's the new occupation of the world.

YASMIN: He followed me to work. He must have followed me back to Brian's one day and then gone round later and threatened him.

JOSH: Right.

YASMIN: Recently my brother's been… (*She looks at JOSH.*) Forget it. I'm a bit drunk.

JOSH: It's fine. Whatever.

YASMIN: And my dad can't cope. He doesn't know where he went wrong. I mean he wants us to be British, but in the same breath would say things like 'Remember you're a Muslim. You'll never be English.' I don't know why I told you that.

JOSH: Uhm…well maybe…

YASMIN: I mean I've noticed, you know, the English, they have kids and they think 'Right, now, my job is to make them happy and everything', but of course, you know, they'll fuck it up one way or the other. With my lot, it's the kids that have to make the parents happy and we'll definitely fuck that up. So basically we're all fucked.

JOSH: Parents. Who needs them?

YASMIN: My mum right, if I don't go and see mum in Barnet at least once a week, she starts quoting the Koran. 'Heaven lies under the feet of one's mother,' she goes. 'You know what that means Yasmin? If you don't visit your mother, you'll go to hell.'

JOSH: My mum's not quite as overt, but she'd quietly nod at the sentiment. (*Beat.*) Barnet's a bit of a trek, isn't it?

YASMIN: It's fucking miles away.

JOSH: Well I'll… I'll just go to the little boys'…

JOSH exits. YASMIN sighs and sips her drink. Enter TARIQ.

YASMIN: Oh shit.

TARIQ: Look at you.

YASMIN: Fucking hell, Tariq.

TARIQ: Don't you have any shame?

YASMIN: Not here, OK?

TARIQ: I don't give a bollocks about these people.

YASMIN: I do.

TARIQ: What's that you're drinking?

YASMIN: Nothing. Leave me alone.

TARIQ: What is it?

YASMIN: Nothing. Just lemonade. Go home.

TARIQ picks up the drink and sniffs it then glares at YASMIN.

TARIQ: You're coming home with me!

YASMIN: Fuck off, Tariq.

TARIQ: Come now.

YASMIN: No. Leave me alone.

TARIQ picks up the bottle of beer.

TARIQ: Whose is this?

YASMIN: I…

TARIQ: Whose beer is this?

YASMIN: It's… I don't know…it was there.

TARIQ: Liar.

YASMIN: It's a bar. People leave things…

TARIQ: He's here, isn't he?

YASMIN: No.

TARIQ: I thought I made it clear to that Brian bloke to keep away.

YASMIN: You did. You ruined my evening.

TARIQ: Then whose beer is this? You've been picking up men like a whore. Look at you. Look at the way you're dressed. It's desperate.

YASMIN: Fuck off will you Tariq? Will you fuck off?

TARIQ: You think I like to be here?

YASMIN: Then go.

TARIQ: This place makes me sick.

YASMIN: You make me sick!

TARIQ: Whose fucking beer is this?!

JOSH enters. YASMIN starts and TARIQ sees him.

JOSH: Is everything all right?

YASMIN: Josh, go away.

JOSH: What?

TARIQ: Who the fuck is this?

YASMIN: Tariq, don't…

TARIQ: Who the fuck are you?

JOSH: Who the fuck are you?

TARIQ: Fuck off, geezer, I don't know you innit.

JOSH: Is this guy bothering you?

YASMIN: Josh.

TARIQ: Josh?

YASMIN: It's my brother.

TARIQ: Josh? Joshua? That a Jewish name?

JOSH: What if it is?

TARIQ shoves JOSH.

Do that again.

TARIQ: I don't know you.

JOSH: Touch me again.

TARIQ: Piss off yeah.

JOSH: Push me again and see what happens.

YASMIN: Both of you stop it!

JOSH: I mean who the fuck do you think you are?

TARIQ: He's a Jew innit.

YASMIN: Both of you fucking stop it now!

TARIQ: You fucking keep away from my sister man. I swear…

JOSH: You've got a problem have you?

TARIQ: You're the fucking problem Jewboy.

JOSH slaps TARIQ.

YASMIN: Josh!

TARIQ takes a swing at JOSH. JOSH dodges the swing and grabs TARIQ's arm. JOSH knocks TARIQ's wrist with his knee forcing TARIQ to drop the bottle, then he knees TARIQ in the stomach. As TARIQ clutches his stomach, YASMIN grabs JOSH's arm and pulls him away.

Leave him alone!

While JOSH is looking at YASMIN, TARIQ picks up the bottle.

He's my brother.

TARIQ smashes the bottle over JOSH's head. JOSH falls to his knees clutching his head.

No!

Darkness. Silence.

Lights up on JOSH on his knees holding his head. YASMIN and TARIQ have gone. OFFICER comes over and kneels to help JOSH to his feet. JOSH gets up, dazed.

OFFICER: You were given information over the radio.

JOSH: Please...

OFFICER: You were told...

JOSH: Let me sleep.

OFFICER: You were told...come on...you were told...

JOSH: What do you want from me?

OFFICER: You were told that a homicide bomber was captured alive.

JOSH: You know this.

OFFICER: You were told she was going to detonate herself up in an ice-cream parlour full of kids.

JOSH: Yes. Look...

OFFICER: You were told...come on!

JOSH: What? I...

OFFICER: You were told her boyfriend – Yusef Abu Toameh – was a captain of the Al Aqsa Martyrs and involved in masterminding the attack.

JOSH: Yes.

OFFICER: You were told that Yusef Abu Toameh fitted the description of the man you were holding.

JOSH: Yes. Yes. Yes.

OFFICER: You were told he must be captured alive!

JOSH: Yes. Yes. OK? Let me sleep!

OFFICER: Don't you understand! I could keep you here till we give back Jerusalem! I could never let you sleep! Never! Now talk to me! Tell me why you did it!

The lights change again. We are back on the dust road on the West Bank.

JOSH: (*On walkie-talkie.*) How long will that be? (*Burble.*) But he's not carrying any weapon. He says he just went out to get a newspaper. (*Burble.*) What? I don't know if he's lying? (*Burble.*) How do you know he's lying? (*Burble.*) OK. I will. Bye.

JOSH puts down the walkie talkie.

YUSEF: I hate to trouble you.

JOSH glares at YUSEF.

JOSH: What?

YUSEF: Do you have any idea how long this is going to take?

JOSH: What have I told you?

YUSEF: No just…

JOSH: Just…

YUSEF: I only ask because…

JOSH: Just sit there. Just fucking sit there. Just sit there and keep still and keep silent and I won't have to shoot you in the face. OK?

Silence.

YUSEF: It's just that I've got a date.

JOSH: Excuse me?

YUSEF: Just a cup of coffee.

JOSH: You've got a what?

YUSEF: I've been tying to persuade her for months.

JOSH: *You* have a date?

YUSEF: She finally caved.

JOSH: With an actual girl?

YUSEF: I went on the charm offensive.

JOSH: I don't believe this.

YUSEF: You want to know the secret?

JOSH: Excuse me?

YUSEF: There's only one secret worth knowing in this world, didn't your father tell you that?

JOSH: My father kept his secrets close to his chest.

YUSEF: Well there is only one secret worth knowing and that is how to get a woman into bed. (*Beat.*) So you want to know it?

JOSH: All right. We'll do this. What's the secret?

YUSEF: Flattery.

JOSH: (*Beat.*) That's it? That's the big earth-shattering discovery…

YUSEF: What? No good?

JOSH: That's your secret? Flattery? That's it?

YUSEF: Simple I know, but effective.

JOSH: I thought you Arabs had your women under control.

YUSEF: What?

JOSH: Yeah, that's right…

YUSEF: Under control? Our women? Are you insane man?

JOSH: That's what I hear.

YUSEF: They're a particular breed, Palestinian girls. You ever tried chatting up a Palestinian girl?

JOSH: That may be the most absurd thing you've said so far.

YUSEF: This… I mean…this particular girl. Oh she… I don't know what it is about her, but I just…and take my word for it I'm the biggest coward on the planet, but I'll risk those checkpoints and that curfew for one of her dimply grins. For one kiss from her long lips. (*Beat.*) Are you married?

JOSH: I'm not sharing my marital status or any other private information with you.

YUSEF: Not married. OK. Girlfriend?

JOSH: Look…listen…

YUSEF: OK. No girlfriend. But you've had girlfriends, right? I mean…

JOSH: Of course I've had girlfriends. Of course I've had girlfriends.

YUSEF: OK. OK. Let's change the subject. Let's talk about something else. Uh...Religion? No. Politics? Better not.

JOSH: Listen, I want to ask you a question.

YUSEF: Geography!? No. History!? No. No good.

JOSH: I want to...what is it with you talking all the time?

YUSEF: Sex was a good one you see.

JOSH: Do you – do you – I mean do you have a disease or something?

YUSEF: Sex is neutral. Sex is universal.

JOSH: Do you have some kind of disorder?

YUSEF: Nerves. I'm nervous. I'm just nervous. I have to talk when I'm nervous.

JOSH: Nerves?

YUSEF: I'm tied up and blindfolded and you have a gun. That'll just about do it. Plus you threaten me and hit me occasionally and that doesn't help the anxiety.

JOSH: You are the ache in my fucking arse.

YUSEF: Thank you.

JOSH: What do you think would happen if I shot you right now? Huh? If I just got bored of waiting here for my superiors and turned this M-16 on you and fired? You think anything would happen to me? I'd just say you tried to escape. Nothing would happen to me. This is *war*. We're fighting a *war*. No-one would do anything to me, there would be no consequences, the world wouldn't cry out in disgust, it would keep on spinning exactly as it has been. I could end it now. I could end your miserable existence right now. Then you wouldn't worry about how to get women to like you because you'd be dead! Do you hear what I'm saying? I could stamp out your life like a garden snail and it would mean absolutely fucking NOTHING!!

Pause.

YUSEF: My name is Yusef by the way. Yusef Abu Toameh. What's yours?

JOSH: I'm not telling you my name.

YUSEF: Why not?

JOSH: Because…

YUSEF: What's in a name?

JOSH's radio burbles.

JOSH: Shalom. (*Burble.*) Sir… I have… (*Burble.*) I receive that. (*Burble.*) She? (*Burble.*) Yes. (*Burble.* Beat.) Sir, I think it's unlikely… (*Burble.*)

Pause. JOSH looks at YUSEF.

JOSH: Could you repeat that name, sir? (*Burble.*) Yes sir. (*Beat.*) Thank you.

Pause. JOSH stares at YUSEF, who has frozen.

Lights fade to black.

ACT THREE

Scene 1

Bedroom. Dark. SARA and the WAITER crash into the room kissing wildly.

SARA: Come on.

SARA pulls WAITER on to the bed. They pull each other's clothes off. WAITER gets on top of SARA and they writhe around, groaning.

WAITER: Hang on.

SARA: What?

WAITER: Is it in?

SARA: What?

WAITER: Is my cock in?

SARA: No.

WAITER: Shit.

SARA: You're way off.

WAITER: Sorry.

SARA: Oaw. Don't poke at it?

WAITER: Shit, sorry.

WAITER pulls away.

Sorry.

SARA: What?

WAITER: I'm sorry.

SARA: For Christ's sake.

WAITER: I'm sorry I just can't.

SARA: Jesus.

WAITER: I'm sorry. I think I just…

SARA switches a lamp on. And searches for her cigarettes.

Fuck.

Pause. SARA stares at the waiter. She is almost about to laugh.

SARA: I just realised something.

WAITER: What?

SARA: I forgot your name.

WAITER: Oh.

SARA: Huh.

SARA offers WAITER a cigarette, but he shakes his hand to decline. SARA lights up, smokes.

WAITER: It's Brian.

SARA: What?

WAITER: My name.

SARA: Oh.

WAITER: Hello.

SARA: I'm Sara.

WAITER: I know.

SARA: We were going to fuck and I couldn't even remember your name.

WAITER: Yeah. F-funny.

SARA: Oh, but it's probably best that we didn't…

WAITER: Yeah. Probably.

SARA: Brian. Look. We had a lot to drink.

WAITER: Yeah. Yeah. We did. You got a bog?

SARA: Straight through, end of the landing.

WAITER exits. SARA smokes and thinks back. There is a lighting change.

JOSH enters and climbs into bed with SARA and they kiss.

Hello you.

JOSH kisses SARA's neck.

Thanks for dinner.

JOSH: You're welcome.

SARA: I felt very special.

JOSH: Remember Rodney and Caroline's wedding?

SARA: A year ago today.

JOSH: Yup.

SARA: I'm not going to forget our first kiss in a hurry.

JOSH: I was pretty smooth, wasn't I?

SARA: (*Laughs.*) Smooth?!

JOSH: From what I recall.

SARA: From what I recall you were so nervous about your speech you had to hold on to something to stay standing. And that something was me.

JOSH: You see my recollection of it is that I swept you off your feet.

SARA: Oh really.

JOSH: (*Significantly.*) Sara.

JOSH climbs out of the bed.

SARA: You look like you've got something significant to say.

JOSH goes to look through his trousers pocket from something.

Josh. You're making me nervous.

JOSH: Just a minute.

SARA: You know I don't like surprises. You know they make me testy.

JOSH: Just have a bit of patience.

SARA: You know, like when there are crumbs in your bed when you're trying to sleep. Or when I find your socks in my bed when I'm trying to get comfy.

JOSH finds it and checks it. His back is to SARA who can't see what he is doing.

JOSH: Here it is.

SARA: Which reminds me. I found one of your socks in my bed the other day.

JOSH: I haven't lost any socks.

SARA: Yeah. (*Pulling the sock from her bedside drawer.*) Here it is.

JOSH: (*Holding a ring box.*) Sara.

SARA: Really Joshua, it's a bit childish to have socks with Fred Flintstone on them.

JOSH: What?

SARA: I mean who bought you these, your mum or something? (*Suddenly seeing the ring box.*) What's that?

JOSH: Did you say Fred Flintstone?

SARA: Oh my God is that what I think it is?

JOSH: Fuck. Show me that.

JOSH grabs the sock roughly.

SARA: What's the matter with you?

JOSH: This.

SARA: Josh.

JOSH: This…it's not mine.

Beat.

SARA: Oh. I…

JOSH: Jesus.

SARA: I…no…I…

JOSH: What have you done?

SARA: Oh God.

JOSH: What have you done Sara?

SARA: Josh.

JOSH: This is Chris's sock. I know. I know because…

SARA: Shit.

JOSH: He won it for…at the…he won it for…

SARA: Oh no. Not like this.

JOSH: Dancing the…Did you f… Sara, did you sleep with Chris?

Pause.

You…I…

SARA: I'm sorry.

JOSH: How? When?

SARA: When you were…it doesn't matter…

JOSH: Just answer the fucking question!

SARA: We just got drunk one night. You…you insisted on getting us together. You kept going on about how much we'd get on. You kept banging on about how we should get to know each other.

JOSH: So you fucked him!

SARA: Josh…

JOSH: THAT'S TAKING IT A TAD FUCKING LITERALLY, ISN'T IT?!!!

Pause. SARA tries to touch JOSH, but he pulls away.

Why?

SARA: What?

JOSH: Why?

SARA: I… I don't… I told you…we…we went to that bar…we were waiting for you. You never showed up.

JOSH: I had to work.

SARA: You were suffocating me, Josh. All this stuff about the future, about moving to Israel, and now this…this is fucking typical of you. You go and get a ring. You… I bet you asked my Dad for permission before asking me, didn't you?

JOSH: (*Beat.*) I…

SARA: You did, didn't you?

JOSH: That's really no excuse for fucking my best friend.

SARA: Yeah, I know that, but you do this. You push. You don't ask if it's what I want. You just go ahead with your plans and you treat me like I'm your little pet, your little puppy and I'm sick of it.

JOSH: So I make you sick. Is that it? I make you sick?

SARA: I didn't say that…

JOSH: But you meant it. And now the feeling's mutual.

SARA: Josh!

JOSH goes.

Shit.

WAITER returns. Lights change.

WAITER: I want to say something.

SARA: (*Distracted.*) What?

WAITER: I have something to say.

SARA: Really. You don't have to.

WAITER: But I want to.

SARA: It honestly doesn't matter.

WAITER: I feel as though I misrepresented myself.

SARA: Don't worry about it.

WAITER: No, but I don't feel I was at my best.

SARA: Quite.

WAITER: I mean you can't expect a bloke to perform at full stretch when he's totally trolleyed. I mean you can knock back the wine. I was trying to keep up with you.

SARA: We didn't have that much.

WAITER: But red wine. I mixed the grape and the grain, that's what's done me in.

SARA: I'm sure under normal conditions you're a stallion.

WAITER: If you like. I mean I've had no complaints before. I've... I've always been a solid campaigner. And I feel... I've let myself down.

SARA: I told you it's fine.

WAITER: But you can't be wholly gratified, can you?

SARA: Not even fractionally.

WAITER: I can't do this. It's a lie.

SARA: What?

WAITER: I'm lying. It has happened before. Several times.

SARA: I don't think I could stomach a candid confession just at the moment.

WAITER: And working in a bar you meet so much totty, you know? I mean Friday night it's wall-to-wall scranny. It's a veritable honey pot as far as quim goes. Straight up.

SARA: I can't tell you how pleased I am for you.

WAITER: Right. But my willy seems to have a mind of its own. It won't step up when it's given the green light. It can see it's being waved up in, but it's...shy.

SARA: Shy? I don't think I've ever heard of a shy prick before.

WAITER: I mean I enter into the contract in good faith, I'll come back to hers or her to mine, we'll grope for a bit... I know you lot like to call that foreplay...and then when it comes to the crucial moment...it back-pedals.

SARA: Really, this is a beautiful story, but I have to get up horribly early... I have to get to the airport.

WAITER: Oh? Going on hols?

SARA: Work.

WAITER: Yeah. So anyway there was one girl. Yasmin. I met her in hospital. My Nan just had a new hip put in. Yas was so kind. It was the kindness that made me fall for her. That and the starched uniform. I was due to meet her tonight, but her brother put a stop to it.

SARA: Look…

WAITER: Fucking Pakis.

SARA: … Pardon me?

WAITER: That's what he was. Yasmin's brother.

SARA: Look…listen… I have to get a plane in the morning… I…

WAITER: I mean she's feminine and delicate and vulnerable. I mean she's not the type to just jump into bed with some bloke she hardly knows. She's decent.

SARA: Excuse me, excuse me, is that meant to be…

WAITER: Oh no…no I didn't mean…look I mean you're a sexy chick, you know, I bet there's a lot of guys want to slot it in.

SARA: Well I'm charmed.

WAITER: I was due to see her tonight and this Tariq, he comes round my house. Talks to me like I'm filth. Threatens my mum!

SARA: Oh right, you live with your mum. Well…

WAITER: My mum is a churchgoer for Christ's fucking sake, (*Burps.*) she don't need the aggravation. And this Tariq, yeah, he starts fucking ranting and raving like the whole fucking world's on fire. I mean who the fuck do these people think they are, yeah? They come here… this…this country. Abuse our hospitality.

SARA: OK, I think we're just about done here.

WAITER: You see the benefit system…yeah…works in their favour yeah? If you got a whole fucking bucket load of kids…don't matter you're not actually *English.* That you can't speak a word of *English.*

SARA: Can we do this some other time, do you think?

WAITER: See they're laughing at us. Fuck. They come here with their backward culture, I mean look, don't get me wrong, I know it's not a (*Burps.*) a picnic where they come from, but is that our fault? Is that my fucking fault? I know they live in a shit hole, but don't bring your muck over here! Because…they ain't got no loyalty to this country. We let 'em in and now…they're telling us how to live. Fucking…blowing shit up. And I know what you're thinking. You're thinking I'm a racialist, but you see that's nothing to do with it…no you're mis…mis…you're misunderst…you don't get it. No, see I'm prepared to shag any girl. Any race, creed or colour, yeah? I don't discriminate, yeah? So how can I be a racialist if I'm prepared to shag a Paki? Answer me that.

SARA: …it's Brian isn't it?

WAITER: You see it in people, you feel it rising in people you know, they've…they've had enough, yeah? I see it happening. We're a soft touch, right? But there's only so much we can take. So I'm telling you and I'm being fucking serious about this. They'll get theirs. Because we're a proud nation. And we're hard…we're fucking hard…underneath.

Silence.

SARA: I've got the number of a cab firm. (*Silence.*) I think this was a mistake.

WAITER: Yeah. A cab. Yeah.

SARA: We made a mistake.

WAITER: Put it down to experience, yeah?

SARA: Try not to wake your mum up when you get in. Sounds like she's had a rough night.

WAITER: Wait, can't we just… Could you… I just want to… I just want you to…could you…

SARA: What?

WAITER: Hold me?

SARA: Oh.

WAITER: Give me a sort of a hug.

SARA: I…

WAITER: Just…

Silence. SARA doesn't move. WAITER withers.

SARA: I should phone that cab.

Darkness.

Scene 2

YASMIN's flat. YASMIN examines TARIQ's hand.

TARIQ: 'Kin hell woman!

YASMIN: You've got a piece of glass in here.

TARIQ: It hurts.

YASMIN: Keep still.

TARIQ: Ah.

YASMIN: I said keep still.

TARIQ: Get it out.

YASMIN: You might have to go to hospital.

TARIQ: I'm not going to no stinking hospital, innit.

YASMIN: You're so stubborn.

TARIQ: Just get it out, bitch!

YASMIN: I'll let you bleed to death, you speak to me like that.

TARIQ: You wouldn't do that.

YASMIN: Then you'd be in paradise. Then you could be with all your virgins.

Beat. YASMIN gets cleaning stuff and cotton wool and starts to clean the wound.

Oh. What if alcohol got in your blood stream from tonight? Would that scupper your chances?

YASMIN pushes a little too hard.

TARIQ: (*Howling in pain.*) Fuck!

YASMIN: It's out.

TARIQ: *Jesus, Mary and Joseph.*

YASMIN: I have to clean it. Wait.

TARIQ looks pained.

TARIQ: That geezer's a cocksucker innit.

YASMIN: You're the cocksucker. You started it. He was totally innocent.

TARIQ: Yeah right. He was on the pull man.

YASMIN: He's the son of a patient. Idiot. You always go leaping to conclusions. You're such a prick sometimes.

TARIQ: Patient?

YASMIN: You know the writer I told you about. Max Pepper.

TARIQ: Yasmin…

YASMIN: He told me…he made me promise not to give him…

TARIQ: Yasmin, I want to tell you something.

YASMIN: But I talked to him tonight. (*TARIQ is about to start again.*) No Tariq wait. We talked about Dad.

TARIQ: You talked about Dad with *him*?

YASMIN: And I can't help thinking…all he wants is to be like him. But his Dad won't let him.

TARIQ: You keep family business to yourself. You hear me.

YASMIN: But it reminded me of you. And how you used to want to do everything Dad did. And he never let you. Always pushing you to be… I don't know…just…

TARIQ: I spoke to Khalid.

Pause.

YASMIN: Our cousin Khalid?

TARIQ: He phoned me.

YASMIN: Khalid phoned you?

TARIQ: I'm going to Pakistan.

YASMIN: Tariq no…

TARIQ: There's so much happening. So much I can learn. I need to be part of it.

YASMIN stops and throws away the bloodied swabs.

I need to follow my destiny. I don't fit here. I never did. Not really. Now I know what has to be done. I've got something to fight for. Do you…do you understand?

YASMIN: Oh what is this bullshit you keep spouting about destiny?

TARIQ: My destiny as a Muslim.

YASMIN: Fuck off then.

TARIQ: When a Muslim is attacked, that's an attack on all of us. It's an attack on Allah.

YASMIN: Go on, go out there and start World War Three. It's your destiny.

TARIQ: You think I should care about football and Britney's arse when the fucking world's on fire!?

YASMIN: I just want my brother back.

TARIQ: Thousands and thousands of our brothers die. Whole countries ripped apart so the Yanks can control the oil.

YASMIN: Don't go.

TARIQ: And our hearts are supposed to bleed for a handful of white people.

YASMIN: Please. Don't go there. Not there. Not now.

TARIQ: I have to. There's nothing else for me here.

YASMIN: I'm here.

TARIQ: You should be supporting me in this.

YASMIN: What?

TARIQ: We have to stand up for ourselves, Yas.

YASMIN: This is nothing to do with me.

TARIQ: The west are bombing our cities. They're arresting men for having dark skin. Torturing them. Sticking electrodes on their balls.

YASMIN: They're all terrorists.

TARIQ: Who told you? The *Sun*? The Government?

YASMIN: Let the Yanks go to war. Blow them all up. Good. They're a fucking disgrace. Nuke them all.

TARIQ: These are your people…

YASMIN: I'm English. And I'm scared of getting on the tube.

Beat.

Tariq, I wasn't going to do anything with Brian. I swear. I wasn't going to shag him. I was just going to have a drink with him. That's all. I promise.

TARIQ: You watch what happens this century. This is our time. This is the century of Mohammed. Watch.

Darkness.

Scene 3

Cell. OFFICER reads from a book.

OFFICER: 'The Weinsteins were influential in the community. A *frum* family. Their house faced the park. Mum. Dad. Sister. And Weinstein. It was the fifties. Mosley and his Union of blackshirts were stirring up trouble again in the streets round Hackney. Weinstein fell in love with a girl called Nancy. She wasn't Jewish. "Why are you knocking about with that *shiksa*?" his father would ask. What they didn't know was that Nancy's family were fascist supporters. They were members of the party. And Weinstein wanted to be one too.'

Pause.

It's a good story.

JOSH: Glad you enjoyed it.

OFFICER: I like the gang. The Jewish boys. They're funny.

JOSH: Right…

OFFICER: Your father knew this Weinstein?

JOSH: Yes.

OFFICER: He was the one who tied him up?

JOSH: Yes.

OFFICER: They beat him and stripped him?

JOSH: Yes.

OFFICER: They were punishing him? For turning against them?

JOSH: Yes.

OFFICER: But it doesn't say… How did he get off the tree? You don't say. Did he vanish into thin air? Did the blackshirts come and help him. What? What happened in the end? It's so frustrating. You just leave us hanging. I hate that.

JOSH: Sorry.

OFFICER: And it doesn't say what you think.

JOSH: No.

OFFICER: You don't say what you think. You don't say whether it was right or not. Whether he should have been attacked for being an anti-semite.

JOSH: What are you saying?

OFFICER: It's equivocal is what I'm saying.

JOSH: Look…

OFFICER: It does not condemn him.

JOSH: I'm a Jew.

OFFICER: Yes.

JOSH: I'm…

OFFICER: In fact he's not such a bad fellow this Weinstein. He tells jokes. He falls in love.

JOSH: Because he's a young man. He's deluded, he's confused, he's running away from himself…

OFFICER: Yes.

JOSH: But he's not an animal. He's got a soul. It's a mistake…

OFFICER: Yes?

JOSH: I think… I used to think…but I think now it's a mistake to…

OFFICER: Yes.

JOSH: I was trying to…put myself inside his head.

OFFICER: Yes.

JOSH: To see beyond myself. To feel things it isn't possible for me to feel.

OFFICER: But you don't feel them?

JOSH: I'm Jewish. I'm Israeli.

OFFICER: Hmm.

JOSH: I believe… I…

OFFICER: Do you? Do you believe in Israel?

Pause.

JOSH: I burned all my bridges in London. My father died. My mother's angry with me for writing that story. My…there was a girl, but I…

OFFICER: Yes?

JOSH: This is home now. There is nowhere else for me.

Pause.

OFFICER: Tell me about the last time you saw your father.

Hospital room.

JOSH: Hello.

MAX: What happened to your face?

JOSH: Nothing. I fell. A nurse…

MAX: You all right?

JOSH: Fine. Dad. I've been doing some thinking.

MAX: Oh.

JOSH: It's not right that we should feel uncomfortable with each other.

MAX: Uncomfortable? Try having a plastic tube shoved up your Johnson. You don't know the meaning of the word. Look. I've been thinking too. I want you to move back here. Live in my old flat in Hendon. It's not safe out there. Israel's a madhouse. It's no place for a nice Jewish boy.

JOSH: (*Beat.*) It's no madder than anywhere else.

MAX: There's nothing mad about Hendon. Hendon is perfectly sane.

JOSH: Dad…

MAX: I want you to come home. This is not your war.

JOSH: I feel…in England I always feel displaced.

MAX: We're a nomadic people, of course we feel displaced. That's our personality.

JOSH: England's a dead country. It's long, long had its day. There's nothing worth building here, nothing left to believe in but making money. In Israel you're alive every minute. You taste life. We're putting the country together with our hands.

MAX: But it's a country built on prejudice. What's happening to the Palestinians is *Lebensraum*, it's *Lebensraum* Josh, and surely us, the Jews, of all people… how can we…of all people…

JOSH: No. We're not the victims anymore. That's over now.

MAX: Right, now we make victims of other people?

JOSH: I see it like this: you're given a choice, a clear choice. You can go backwards. You can be the victims again or you can be free and strong and have the whole world criticise you. Which would you choose? Wouldn't you say – 'Fuck The World!'?

Beat.

MAX: It comes down to what side you take boy. It's your group against everyone else. You have to take sides. And you've chosen your side. You've chosen to take sides against humanity. And I weep for you.

Pause.

Why did you come here tonight? What do you want?

JOSH: I don't… I heard you were… I don't know I wanted to…

MAX: I don't even know what we have in common any more.

JOSH: Maybe I should never have come back.

Long pause.

MAX: I'm tired. Help me into bed. (*JOSH helps MAX on to the bed.*) Fathers and sons. Looks like they weren't meant to get on in our family.

JOSH: Can I get you anything? A drink of water?

MAX: My dad barely gave me time of day.

JOSH: Granddad loved you.

MAX: He gave me nothing but a cold silence.

JOSH: He gave you his copy of *War and Peace.*

MAX: In Russian. What good was that? I couldn't speak Russian. I'm supposed to glean its meaning from the shape of the words?

JOSH: He'd kept it with him from the *shtetl* in Minsk, to Warsaw and Krakow, he had that book with him when they liberated him from Auschwitz. He kept it.

MAX: I know...

JOSH: Granddad gave you mystery. He gave you a passion for stories.

MAX: I didn't need his stupid book, I just wanted him to look me in the eyes.

JOSH: (*Plumping the pillows.*) Sit up.

MAX: Don't plump the pillows like that.

JOSH: (*Plumping the pillows.*) Didn't he put you on the *Kindertransport*, knowing he might be caught by the SS? Didn't he risk his life for your safety?

MAX: (*Violent.*) I told you to get your filthy mits off those pillows!

JOSH notices some pages slip out from under MAX's pillows.

JOSH: What's this?

MAX: Leave them.

JOSH picks them up and peruses them. MAX tries to swipe the pages, but can't.

Get your hands off my property.

JOSH: Just a moment.

MAX: It's of no interest to you…

JOSH: Is this a story?

MAX: Give them here.

JOSH: Let me read it.

MAX: It's not finished.

JOSH: Your last great opus?

MAX: Josh. Put them down.

JOSH: (*Reading.*) So it's true.

MAX: DAMN YOU, DO AS I SAY!

JOSH: Just a minute.

MAX: I never show my work before it's done.

Beat. MAX reaches for the papers again, but JOSH keeps hold of them. MAX is too weak to fight JOSH, who moves to the side of the room and reads. After a while…

Well.

JOSH: Is this true?

MAX: Does it matter?

JOSH: You don't remember, do you?

MAX: Remember what?

JOSH: My story.

MAX: What story?

JOSH: When I was twelve.

MAX: Twelve?

JOSH: I'd had a fight with my friends.

MAX: Of course I don't remember, that was twenty years ago… Don't be ridiculous.

JOSH: I wanted to write about it. I was working on it for a few days. I slept with the note pad under my pillow for fear the wind would come crashing in through the walls and blow away the pages. I felt as though I was on fire, as though I was soaring. One night, as I was scribbling away you saw my light was on and you came into my room. You asked me what I was doing. I tried to cover up the writing, but you snatched the pad from me and started to read. I begged you… I begged you to stop. I told you I wasn't finished, that it wasn't ready. I pleaded with you, I tried to grab the pages back, but you were too big.

MAX: I…

JOSH: You finished reading. You looked at me. You told me…and I remember it so clearly. You told me… 'This isn't a fit subject for you.'

MAX: Joshua…son, I was trying to…

JOSH: 'This isn't a fit subject for you.'

MAX: Well. Yes. Well. You know.

JOSH: You told me it was backward-looking.

MAX: I was trying to…

JOSH: That it was too complex a subject for a young boy. Who shouldn't be concerned with that sort of…

MAX: …yes… I was trying to teach you.

JOSH: …with tribal identity…

MAX: Toughen you up. To…to…

JOSH: …with our collective guilt.

MAX: Sons always need to be greater than their fathers. It's evolution.

JOSH: And yet you're writing about what you did to Weinstein.

MAX: Yes but that's different.

JOSH: Isn't that story about our collective guilt?

MAX: No. It's about my guilt. And it's no-one else's business to interfere.

JOSH: No?

MAX: No. Not Sam's. Not yours. No-one's.

JOSH: Like you interfered with my story?

MAX: I'm your father.

JOSH: Like you took the pages of my story…

MAX: Josh. I'm warning you.

JOSH: …and did this…

JOSH holds up the pages. Slowly and deliberately, JOSH tears the pages.

Silence.

MAX: Get out.

JOSH: Dad…

MAX: No. We're finished. I want you to leave. And I never want to see you again.

JOSH stares. Silence.

OFFICER steps out of the darkness.

OFFICER: You were given the order to hold the captive named Yusef Abu Toameh.

JOSH: Yes.

OFFICER: You were told he was seen many times with the homicide bomber we caught with explosives outside the ice cream parlour.

JOSH: Yes.

OFFICER: You were informed he was suspected of planning the attack.

JOSH: Yes.

OFFICER: What happened then?

Enter YUSEF. He falls to his knees. OFFICER fades.

YUSEF: I know this doesn't look good.

JOSH: Don't try to escape.

YUSEF: I can explain.

JOSH: If you try to escape, I will shoot you.

YUSEF: Shoot me?

JOSH: I will shoot you in the leg.

YUSEF: Please…listen…

JOSH: It seems you're needed alive.

YUSEF: Alive. They suspect me?

JOSH: Sit tight.

YUSEF: What will they do to me?

JOSH: That's not my concern.

YUSEF: Please.

JOSH: They'll ask you a few questions.

YUSEF: And what else?

JOSH: I don't know…they'll…

YUSEF: I'm innocent. I had nothing to do with any of this…

JOSH: I hear differently.

YUSEF: You hear wrong.

JOSH: Then you have nothing to worry about.

YUSEF: OK. OK. I'll tell you. I'll tell you the truth.

Lighting change. SAMIRA enters.

SAMIRA: You won't get me to agree, Yusef.

YUSEF: I'll tell you what happened.

JOSH steps back into the darkness.

SAMIRA: You won't get me to change my mind. I've seen what goes on here with these eyes. I don't need you to tell me.

YUSEF: All I'm saying is instead of going to that meeting, come out with me.

SAMIRA: And do what? Go to the Ritz?

YUSEF: We can get ice cream. We can sit under the stars and eat it and talk and maybe…you know…if you're in the mood…we can…you know…fondly grope each other.

SAMIRA: You shouldn't even be in this area. You will get into trouble.

YUSEF: OK. I'm being forward. You can keep most of your clothes on this first time.

SAMIRA: You're always trying it on with me.

YUSEF: Because you make me shake with lust, is that such a crime?

SAMIRA: Be quiet.

YUSEF: I can't help it. Sometimes when things get too hard to bear. When there's no food or no water and we're stuck inside, the whole family huddled together for days and we don't know if the Apache helicopters are going to destroy the house over our heads, I just repeat your name softly to myself. Samira. Samira.

SAMIRA: Typical useless Yusef.

YUSEF: I'm not useless.

SAMIRA: What good are you to anyone? Huh? Huddled up like a frightened animal waiting to be slaughtered?

YUSEF: I keep up morale.

SAMIRA: Don't make me laugh.

YUSEF: I do magic tricks.

SAMIRA: You and your stupid tricks.

YUSEF: I tell jokes. Like…you know… So I said to the gym instructor, 'Can you teach me to do the splits?' And he said, 'How flexible are you?' And I said, 'I can't make Tuesdays'.

SAMIRA: That stinks.

YUSEF: Or…or… OK, a falafel walks into a bar, the barman says, 'I'm sorry, we don't serve food'.

SAMIRA: It makes me want to weep.

YUSEF: I… I sing.

SAMIRA: You're tone deaf.

YUSEF: Stop putting me down OK, I'm just trying to help. I'm trying to help in this hell hole.

SAMIRA: It's pathetic.

YUSEF: Oh what do you want me to do? Charge at the Israelis like your crazy brother?

SAMIRA: Don't you talk about Mahmood.

YUSEF: Hurl myself at one of their tanks and get myself killed? What use is that to anyone?

SAMIRA glares at YUSEF.

I'm sorry. I'm sorry Samira. Forgive me.

SAMIRA: Mahmood is *shahid*. I watched him… I watched them shoot him like an animal in the street. And you think it's something to make fun of?

YUSEF: Please Samira, I was angry, I wasn't thinking…

SAMIRA: Angry? You don't know anger like I do. You don't know rage.

YUSEF: Please…don't go to that meeting.

SAMIRA: You take their side?

YUSEF: I don't take anyone's side except my own. And yours. If you want me to.

SAMIRA: You have to stop with that fawning, Yusef, it's making me sick.

Pause.

YUSEF: Samira…

SAMIRA: I have to go.

YUSEF: What can I say that will stop you?

SAMIRA: Say that there are no more Israelis. Say we can have our country back. Say that all the Jews have gone back to where they came from and we can go home. Say we don't have to live here anymore under this curfew. Say my grandmother can go to the place she was born and my baby brother can be proud of who he is. Say there's hope.

YUSEF can't. SAMIRA leaves.

YUSEF: Samira…

JOSH comes forward. Lighting change.

I should have stopped her. But I went home first to check on my father. Then I realised she might be serious and I ran around trying to find her. I was telling people I was her boyfriend and that they should find me. I told them we were supposed to get married. When people laughed at me, I… I told them… I told them… I was from the Al Aqsa Martyrs. I told them I had changed the plan, and that she had to contact me immediately. But I was too late.

Beat.

JOSH: How do I know you're telling the truth?

YUSEF: I… I don't know…

JOSH: Exactly.

Pause.

YUSEF: You could look in my eyes.

JOSH: What?

YUSEF: Look into my eyes. Decide then if you think I'm lying.

Pause. JOSH stares at YUSEF.

Lights up on SAM who is dressed in black. Sound of mournful Jewish music. SAM puts his hand on JOSH's shoulder. We are at a cemetery.

SAM: Son. Let's go back to the house.

JOSH: You know what his last words to me were?

SAM: Don't. He loved you.

JOSH: I really messed it up.

SAM: He was a difficult man. Don't drive yourself *sedrait* over it.

JOSH: I read some of his story. About Weinstein.

SAM: Let's go back to the house.

JOSH: I wanted to ask you: the end…

SAM: Old news.

JOSH: Somebody took him off that tree.

SAM: Yes.

JOSH: Who?

SAM: I couldn't tell him. I could never tell him.

JOSH: It was you, wasn't it? You let him go.

SAM stares at JOSH. He smiles.

What?

SAM: You reminded me of him just then.

JOSH: Of dad?

SAM: That look. The sudden flash of inspiration.

JOSH: Sam…

SAM: You've got to understand something: Weinstein was my friend. We used to play on the rubble of the houses they bombed on Mare Street. We played war. Max wouldn't play with us. He didn't like getting dirty. He told us he was writing, but I found out he was actually busy trying to get into Hettie Finkelstein's knickers.

SAM chuckles. JOSH winces.

And you want to know the truth about Weinstein? He was dodgy. He wasn't just an innocent victim in all this. He started flirting with the idea of fascism. Yeah. Mixing with these neo-nazi types. Giving them inside information, telling them about soft targets, distributing leaflets talking of a Jewish conspiracy. My life. So you see, we were right to make an example of him. I still stand by that. He needed to be…taught. It's just…just, I couldn't see him suffer. Like I say… I knew him a bit. Anyway that night…the night we did it… I crept out the house…and I got a stepladder – I had to nick one from the *goyisher* family at number thirty two – Jews don't have stepladders – and I helped Weinstein down. He was looking at me… I'd not seen a look like that before. The disgust in his eyes. The hate. I said… 'Sorry mate.' You know what he does? He spits in my face. Then he walks off, brushing himself down as he went.

Beat.

I could never tell anyone. I felt ashamed. I couldn't hold my nerve. Anyway…like I said. Weinstein was my friend. We played war.

Pause.

JOSH: I would have liked to have done something he would have been proud of. Just once.

SAM goes. YASMIN comes over. She is dressed in black.

YASMIN: Hi.

JOSH: (*Surprised.*) Hi.

YASMIN: Thought I'd…pay my…you know…

JOSH: Right. He'd have liked that.

YASMIN: You think?

JOSH: I think he liked you.

YASMIN: He used to bark at me. Used to bite my head off for every little thing.

JOSH: Exactly. That's how he expressed affection.

YASMIN: Right.

Beat. JOSH touches the scar on his face.

Sorry about…my brother…

JOSH: Forget it. Makes me look rugged.

YASMIN: Not really.

JOSH: Oh.

YASMIN: I've got something for you.

She pulls out a manuscript from her bag and hands it to JOSH.

It's the thing he was working on. He'd been sticking the torn pages back together when they found him. I finished it.

JOSH: Oh.

YASMIN: I thought you should have it.

JOSH: Thanks.

YASMIN turns to go.

Wait. Did you read it?

YASMIN: Yeah. It's all right. Needs work on the ending.

YASMIN goes. Enter SARA.

JOSH: I thought you'd gone.

SARA: Cancelled my flight. I liked Max.

JOSH: Yeah. You would.

SARA: Do you think we'll be friends?

JOSH: Probably not. Too tricky.

SARA: Yeah. We should probably avoid each other.

JOSH: Definitely.

SARA: Like kids in a playground who don't get on…

JOSH: Separate them.

SARA: Be best I think.

JOSH: Me too.

Beat.

So when you going back?

SARA: Actually… I'm not.

JOSH: You're not?

SARA: I decided to change posts. I'm staying here.

JOSH: Did your date go particularly well the other night or something?

SARA smiles ruefully.

SARA: Uhm. No. No I just think…I get the feeling there's going be a lot to write about here. Things are changing here.

Pause.

JOSH: Yeah.

Pause.

I had this dream last night. We're all in this café. Me and Mum and Dad. You're there with your parents. Chris is there.

SARA: Chris?

JOSH: Yeah. I know. And I'm all dressed in my full uniform. I'm tooled up you know? Ready. But I'm relaxed and everyone's laughing and having a good time. Anyway then this guy comes in. And I spot him because he's sweating and he's wearing this big coat – one of those parkas with the furry hoods – but it's summer, you know, it's baking and the sun's really bright, so it looks…not suspicious, just…out of place. But what's weirder is he looks familiar. I feel like I know him. You know? Anyway his eyes are staring. Mainly he looks scared, terrified of something. I look at him and I know something bad's going to happen. I know, because I feel it, I know he's got a bomb strapped to his body under that coat. So I get up. But I feel helpless. I know I can't protect you. I want to. All I can think of doing is protecting you all. And he's looking at me. And I'm glaring into his black eyes. And the odd thing is I… I feel this sort of…love. It's weird, all I want to do is put my arms around him. And I do. I squeeze him. And I feel his terror. And I wake up. But the fear stays with me.

SARA: Bye Josh.

SARA goes. YUSEF appears.

YUSEF: What are you going to do?

Pause.

Hello.

JOSH whips out a knife.

JOSH: Now.

JOSH kneels down to join YUSEF. JOSH holds the knife next to YUSEF's face. Then, in one swift movement, he cuts the blindfold off so that they are eye to eye. JOSH and YUSEF regard each other for a while.

Suddenly YUSEF barges into JOSH, knocking him to the floor. YUSEF tries to run away but JOSH leaps on him and tackles him to the floor.

YUSEF: No!

JOSH then starts to pummel YUSEF, beating him and beating him. YUSEF screams out in pain. Then JOSH takes his knife and stands over YUSEF's broken body with a furious look in his eyes. He lifts the knife.

Go on. Kill me. Do it. (*JOSH hesitates.*) I'll be dead! But what will you be?

Lights up. YUSEF has gone.

Blackout. OFFICER comes forward. Gets out a packet of cigarettes.

OFFICER: Cigarette?

JOSH shakes his head.

You should. It's good.

JOSH: I never smoked.

OFFICER: I like it. Makes me feel good. (*Lights up and smokes.*)

JOSH: My friends…the guys I grew up with. They work in banks. In law firms. They play football on a Sunday morning. They worry about their mortgages and what new crap their kids are eating. One of them does magic on the side. Weddings and Bar-mitzvahs. He's good. They buy cars, one got divorced. One of them's a fucking actor, for Christ's sake. He's in an advert for Daz. Fucking Daz. And all he does is moan about not getting seen for things. Being too short or too thin or too hairy.

OFFICER: What is this Daz?

JOSH: And I wonder, you know, I wonder if they're happy. And I wonder… I wonder if they'd have the stomach for all this.

OFFICER: I've grown tired of fighting. We go round in circles here.

Pause. OFFICER drops his cigarette on the floor and stubs it out.

(*Beat.*) You know I never approved of having foreigners in the army. This can never truly be your country.

JOSH: (*Nothing.*)

OFFICER: OK. Let's go over this report again. So I can understand.

Darkness.